RE-INVENT YOURSELF, TAKE CONTROL OF YOUR LIFE.... & MAKE YOUR FIRST MILLION

IN 9 SIMPLE LESSONS

MICHAEL ROSENBLUM

Book Design by HMDPUBLISHING

For My Wife Lisa

Without Whom, I Would Be Worth Nothing

You are playing a giant game of Monopoly. We all are.

We weren't asked if we wanted to play.
We were simply born into it, and to make matters worse, no one ever told us the rules.

So, we just keep throwing the dice and moving our piece around and around the board.

We keep collecting $200 as we pass go.

We keep paying out money to other players when we land on Ventnor or Atlantic Avenue, or God-forbid, Park Place.

By the time we get back to GO, we are almost out of money and now we have to start again.

Around and around we go, like a hamster on a treadmill.

We hope we'll land on Community Chest and get a free hand-out of $100. That will help.

We are always wondering
how did those other people get so rich?

It's because someone told them the rules of the game.

No one told us.

So, now I am telling you how this game is played.

The first rule is, you have to re-invent yourself.

CONTENTS

RE-INVENT YOURSELF

The key to success, not just now, but throughout history, as it turns out, is the act of re-inventing yourself.

We need not be trapped in the life in which we had been born. We can make of ourselves anything we want.

This is the actual key to success – re-invention.

This why Louise Veronica Ciccone became Madonna, why Reginald Kenneth Dwight became Elton John, why Bernard Herschel Schwartz became Tony Curtis, why Peter Parker became Spiderman, why Bruce Wayne became Batman, why Archibald Alexander Leach became Cary Grant.

This has been true throughout history. Siddhartha Gautama became The Buddha; Malcolm Little became Malcolm X; Cassius Clay became Muhammad Ali; Norma Jean Mortensen Baker became Marilyn Monroe; Temujin Uge became Genghis Khan; Mohandas Karamchand Gandhi became The Mahatma.

The list is endless.

You can become anyone you want to be and anything you can imagine, and this is the key to success.

For most of human history, the question of who you are was pretty simple to answer. You were whoever your father was, and he was whoever his father was before him. It was a trap.

If you were born the son of a blacksmith, then you were destined to become a blacksmith. If you were born the son of a serf, then you would spend your life as a serf. There was no escaping your fate. You spent your entire life in your small village, rarely if ever venturing more than a few miles from its borders. This was the only life you knew – it was the only life anyone knew.

If you were born a woman, then you had no options at all. That was how the world worked for quite literally thousands of years.

Now, for the first time in history, you are free to become whomever and whatever you wish to become. This is something that has never happened before, and it is here that our greatest potential lies.

The Internet and social media have really driven this change. As the old *New Yorker* cartoon says, "no one on the Internet knows you're a dog," types the dog. Every influencer on TikTok or Instagram has invented a new persona for themselves that is far removed from the person they started as.

However, few of them actually make any money out of it; and try paying the rent with "Likes."

Instead, I am going to show you both how to re-invent yourself and also to use that power to make millions. And it is the money that will set you free.

WHY MONEY?

I recently read a discussion on social media where people were saying things like:

"There are more important things in life than money."

Or

"Money can't buy you happiness."

These are the kind of things that people with no money say to make themselves feel better about themselves.

Let me tell you right now that those aphorisms are bull.

Money is the most important thing that there is.

It may be true that money can't buy you happiness, but the one thing that money can buy you is freedom – freedom to do what you want, when you want, without having to answer to anyone. Freedom to tell your boss to piss off. Actually, you have no boss. Freedom to live your life exactly the way you want to live it without having to answer to anyone.

That's what money buys. Freedom.

And if that isn't happiness, I don't know what is.

And the pathway to that freedom is re-invention.

ABOUT THIS BOOK

What this is not.

This is NOT a 'Get Rich Quick' book.

I don't have any advice on crypto or borrowing money to buy real estate rental properties, or any one of a hundred other schemes you can find on Amazon or YouTube.

This is a book about learning to see the world and think and live in a different way, and in doing so, both making a lot of money, as well as living a much happier life. It is a book about shedding old beliefs and your old life and re-inventing yourself to become someone you want to be.

And to profit from the transformation, both spiritually and financially.

PART I

LEARNING TO SEE YOURSELF AND THE WORLD IN A NEW WAY

The trick to making your first million – and hopefully more – is to learn to see the yourself and the world in a very different way and to think and act in a different way.

What do I mean by that?

The way you see the your life; the things you believe to be true are, in fact, abstractions. They are simply fictions that you have been educated to believe. But they are not actually true. They are a created or mediated world that you have bought into.

Time to take the red pill.

If you had been born 500 years ago, you would have been a serf.

Back then, everyone was a serf. It was the only way of life that anyone knew. There was nothing else. As a serf, you would have spent your entire life working in the fields for the Lord of the Manor, who owns all the land. You would have spent your days hoeing the dirt or planting seeds by hand or harvesting or tending to his sheep. You would have lived in a rudimentary hut with a dirt floor. If you're a man, your wife would have made the one shirt that you own. Everyone owns one shirt. Most people don't even have shoes. To you, this seems completely normal. This is how you have always lived. This is how everyone you know lives.

To your mind, this is the was the way the world is supposed to be, and on Sundays, the village priest is there to remind you that this is God's given order. Your lot in life is to obey. You are glad to have your little hut and the bits of food you could scrape together and your shirt and your shoes. You should be happy. Yet, in the back of your mind, there is this nagging feeling that something is wrong. You just can't put your finger on it.

Then, one day, a stranger comes into your village.

He looks around at the way you are living and says, he has an idea. He says the shirt your wife made is pretty good. Maybe she could make a few more.

You laugh. "Why should she make another one when I have all I need?"

The stranger says that if she made another one or two, you could take them to the monthly fair in the nearby market town and sell them.

You think about it for a few minutes. "Even if I did that, you say, what do I need with money? I get all the food I need here that we grow for the Lord of the Manor." This stranger seems a troublemaker.

"Well," says the stranger, "You could take the money and buy yourself another sheep."

"And what would I do with another sheep?" you ask. Surely, this man is a fool. Our one sheep provides all the wool we need. And we have to feed it. One sheep is more than enough, thanks.

"Well, you could take that other sheep and make more wool for more shirts and sell those in the market for more money. Then, you could take that money and buy more sheep."

This stranger is even dumber than you thought. "But even if I had three sheep, how many shirts could my wife possibly weave?" you ask.

"Well, you could hire your neighbor's wives and their children to come and work for you weaving shirts, and then take those to the market, and in doing so, buy even more sheep to make more wool to make more shirts. And soon, the whole village would be working for you, and you could have enough money to buy the manor house and you could be the Lord of the Manor."

You might think that the serf would think, 'well, this stranger is pretty smart. He's got some great ideas.' But in fact, this is not what happens. This is dangerous talk. Instead, the stranger is accused of being a witch, of consorting with the devil and trying to overturn the natural God-given order of the world. And so, the visiting stranger is instead bound and burned at the stake.

"So much for that!" you say, and all the villagers have a party and a dance and then go back to gleaning the fields and tending to the Lord's animals.

The stranger's ideas would, in fact, have been pretty easy to do. Any serf could have re-invented themselves as an early capitalist or a Lord of the Manor, but no one did . No one did because everyone was locked into the idea of feudalism and their role in it-even if the seeds for capitalism were always there, waiting to be planted and harvested, it would take another 500 years.

Reading this, you are no doubt thinking, 'ha, if I were that peasant, I would have known exactly what to do'.

This is probably not the case.

In the early 1990's, I formed a company called Video News International. I had 102 reporters all over the world making news stories on their own and selling their work to TV networks. It was a pretty good business; later, I would sell it to The New York Times,

One day, an intern named Anthony Lapee who was working for me (we were based in Philadelphia), said, "Mr. Rosenblum, you gotta meet some guys who are doing something very interesting". So that night, we went over to the Comcast Building. Down in the basement, there were 4 long-haired guys sitting in front of giant CRT screens. Anthony introduced me. "These guys are working on the Internet," he said.

"What is the Internet?" I asked

They explained that as a test program, they had wired up 1500 homes in Philadelphia to get 'The Internet' on their computers. There, they could read newspapers and in this case, watch videos as well.

"Anthony tells us you have like 100 reporters around the world making video stories," they said. I said I did.

"Well, they said, we'd like to put their videos on the Internet so our users can watch them."

This struck me as a dumb idea. Why would you watch TV on your computer when you could watch it on your TV set? But I was here, so I asked, "what are you going to pay me for all this content?"

They took a beat.

"Well, we can't pay anything, but we'll set you up with a web site and give you a URL."

"What's a URL?"

"It's a kind of address so people can find your content. We can make up a nice URL for you, like Broadcast.com, or TV.com or News.com. Whatever you like."

I felt like they were just wasting my time. I passed. Later, Mark Cuban ran with Broadcast.com and sold it to Yahoo for $5.7 billion. So who was the stupid peasant?

The problem, for our peasant, and the problem for you, is not technical or financial, it is psychological.

The potential for you to make your first million is right in front of you, as it was in front of me. You only need to learn to see the world in a slightly different way and then re-invent yourself. This is your pathway to your first million and the security and happiness that that brings.

WHY A MILLION?

There is an old expression that says, 'the first million is the hardest'.

I am not so sure this is true.

It is true that it is hard to earn your first million, but I will tell you what I think is a lot harder. I think it is a lot harder to spend your whole life working for the Lord of the Manor or a weekly paycheck with no prospect of ever accumulating any real wealth or freedom. I think it is a lot harder to get up every morning and go to a job that you may not hate, but certainly don't love and slog it out for a relative pittance. I think it is a lot harder to live in constant fear that at any moment you might get fired and have your whole world turned upside down.

Compared to that, making a million while doing something you love looks a whole lot easier. And it is. And I am going to show you how to do it.

THE QUICK START GUIDE

Every appliance you own probably still comes with a thick instruction manual, but it also generally comes with a one or two-page quick start guide. Most folks just go right to that, so I have written one for this book.

This is a short book about how to make a million dollars.

It's a lot easier to make a million than you might think. A whole lot easier. That's because there are literally trillions of dollars floating around every day, all up for grabs. All you need to do is to get your hands on a measly million and you're done.

But how?

I can only share my own personal experience and pathway to millions with you. There are, no doubt, other ways, but I don't know a damned thing about Bitcoins or investment strategies or rolling mortgages to build a portfolio of rental properties. There are plenty of books about how to do that on Amazon. This one is different. This is a book about learning to think differently.

Learn that, and you can make a million, and probably a whole lot more.

I know. I did. And so, can you.

But to do it, you have to be prepared to re-invent yourself.

WHY I DECIDED TO WRITE THIS BOOK

I was recently an overnight guest at a friend's house.

In the guest room, next to the bed on the night table was a little book; the kind of book that you find in a card shop near the cash register; books with titles like *100 Great Jokes* or *100 Tips for Golfers*. You know, joke books.

The title of this one was, *Make Your Bed*.

Normally, I ignore this kind of stuff, but as luck would have it, my phone was dead and I had left my charger at home, so, as a last resort, I reached for the book. "This should put me to sleep pretty quickly," I thought. Instead, I read it cover to cover.

The book is only 144 pages, and they are little pages. It's by Admiral William H. McRaven, who was a four-star admiral in the US Navy. The book is ten life lessons, mostly gleaned from his experience as a Navy SEAL. I was astonished to learn that the book was at one point #1 on the New York Times Best-seller List, and that he had sold nearly one million copies. That, clearly, is how Admiral McRaven made his million, because you sure don't make that kind of money on a military pension, even if you are an admiral.

I read the book, and it is true that Admiral McRaven has lots of good advice, but it's mostly about, in a sense, following or-ders. I grew up in a military family. I know all about obeying the rules and following orders. I also know all about making your bed first thing in the morning, something with which I heartily agree.

What Admiral McRaven does not touch upon in his book is how to make money. You don't join the military to make a lot of money, but you do get security. Unfortunately, for better or for worse, in our society, which is not about to change all too soon, money is freedom and there is not a lot of job security these days. If you want to become a Navy SEAL, then you should follow all the SEAL rules. But if you want to make a million dollars, you should follow mine.

I have been fortunate in my life. I started relatively poor, but I made money. Not billions, not even hundreds of millions, but enough so that I never had to worry about money again. My father, a not very successful insurance salesman, a job he took after leaving the military, died of a stroke at a relatively early age. He was always filled with stress; stress over money, of which there was never enough. I am sure it was this stress over money that killed him. In fact, I know it was. "Money," he once told me, "should be like hot water. You turn it on when you need it, you turn it off when you're done, and you never have to worry if it's there. It always is."

He never got to that point, and that was what killed him. How much is enough money so that you never have to worry about money again? The number varies from person to person. $5 million? $10 million? But for purposes of this book, I have picked a simple round number. One Million Dollars. If you had a million dollars in your bank account would you be able to stop worrying? I think so.

So, what I am going to do is tell you how to make your first million dollars. It is a lot easier than you probably think it is; but it requires learning to think and work in a totally different and way. It means you may have to break a few "rules", even some of the Admiral's rules.

If I did it, then so can you. Believe me, I was never going to be voted most likely to succeed. When I was in school, I was an utter geek. I carried a fiberglass briefcase. In college, my dorm-mates called me mothball. I didn't learn how to make millions from my father or my family or my education. I had to learn on my own, through a long process of trial and error, but I had a lot of smart people along the way who taught me how to think differently. And that is what I am going to pass on to you – the product of 40 plus years of experience in how to re-invent yourself and in doing so, make real money.

WHAT THIS BOOK IS NOT:

This book is not a 'get rich quick' scheme or any one of a dozen other 'plans' to make money fast. This is about a different way of thinking and interacting with the world. Admiral McRaven's book was subtitled "Positive Thinking in 10 Simple Lessons." Think of this as "How to Make a Million Dollars in 9 Simple Lessons."

PART II

A MILLION DOLLARS IS NOT SO MUCH

A million dollars may seem like a lot of money to you. It is not. It is not going to allow you to buy a mega yacht or a house in the South of France, or for that matter, probably not even a 2-bedroom apartment in Manhattan. What a million dollars is going to buy you is peace of mind. It is going to remove the stress that accompanies everyday life. It means never having to worry about how to pay that credit card bill, or afford the new shoes for the kids, or pay for the heating and electric bill this month, or what if they car needs a major repair. All of the stress, all of the anxiety that has haunted you every day of your life is gone forever. If that isn't happiness, I don't know what is.

When I made my first million dollars, I did something investment counselors would think is idiotic. I put it all into my checking account. Of course, a checking account pays no interest, so that is a dumb thing to do. But it wasn't dumb to me. I put it into my checking account so that I could stop at every ATM machine I passed, put in my card and ask for a total, which I did every day. And there is was. $1,000.000.00, printed right there on the paper that the machine spat out.

Seeing that number in print made me feel at ease, maybe for the first time in my life. Whatever it cost me in interest, it was worth it for the peace of mind it bought me. As your rather typical New Yorker, I had spent endless hours and thousands of dollars in 'therapy'. The day I hit that number, I cancelled my shrink appointments and never looked back. I never had to go back. Amazing, the therapeutic value of a million dollars.

A recent survey by The Federal Reserve reported that an astonishing fifty percent of Americans could not get together $400 if they needed it in an emergency. That is a terrible state of affairs, and it is no way to live. It is also not necessary to live in such stress and fear all the time. A million dollars would free anyone from living under that kind of stress for the rest of their lives.

Fortunately, a million dollars is not all that hard to come by. In fact, it is probably a lot easier than you think. What it requires is learning to see the world in a different way and then learning to act in a different way. This begins with learning to see yourself in a different way, and that is what makes all the difference. It is about having the courage to re-invent yourself. You can do this in 9 Simple Lessons.

But let's start with understanding how much a million dollars is. It may seem an insurmountable amount to acquire, I mean aside from winning the lottery, but in truth it is not. The country and the world for that matter, are awash in money, more than you can possibly imagine. All you need to do to get a million dollars is grab an infinitesimally small bit of it.

How small?

Let's look at it this way. The Gross National Product of the United States is $26.29 Trillion. That's how much money the nation as a whole produces every year. That's a lot of money washing around the economy. To grab a million dollars, you need only get your hands on 0.000000041% of all the money floating around the US. That is nothing. Nothing.

Here's an interesting statistic for you to ponder.

The GNP of the United States is $26,290,000,000,000.00

There are 83,890,000 families in the US.

That means, each family should be earning $313,723.15

Average.

If your family is earning less than $313,723.15 then you are doing something wrong.

In fact, the median income per household in the US is $78,813.00

So where is the rest of all of that money going?

It's up for grabs and it could be yours.

To get just a million dollars, you only need to get your hands on four one-billionths of the yearly GNP.

How small a number is that? Four one-billionths of the GNP. How can you begin to comprehend so small a number our of something so large?

Few of us ever think in terms of billions, unless we are Elon Musk, so here's a good way to think about it:

Let's consider a child's sandbox. It measures 3 meters long, 3 meters wide and is .75 meters deep. There are 5,651 grains of sand per cubic millimeter. The total dimensions of the sandbox, measured in mm are: 1500 x 1500 x 500 = 1,125,000,000 cubic millimeters.

At 5,651 grains of sand per cubic millimeter – there are 6,357,375,000,000 grains of sand in a child's sandbox.

As a representative of the GNP of the United States, each grain of sand represents about $3.50. Each cubic mm is the equivalent of $20K so $1,000,000 is about the equivalent of 282,000 grains of sand, or 50 cubic millimeters. How much is 50 cubic millimeters?

A 50 mm cube measures 4mm x 4mm x 2.5 mm. And how long is 4millimeters? It is the equivalent of 0.157 inches. In other words, it is tiny.

A thimble holds approximately 250 cubic mm of sand. So, we are talking about 1/5th of thimble of sand. About what you might pick up between your toes after a day at the beach and just brush off. That's a million dollars. Nothing. In comparison to the amount of money washing around just in the US, it is nothing.

But our model isn't even limited to the US, because, thanks to the Internet, we now have a global economy. You can just as easily do business in India as you can in Indiana, and all from your home.

And if the GNP of the Unites States is $26.29 Trillion a year, the GNP of the planet is a mind boggling

$134.6 Trillion, or about 6 times that of the US. To grab a cool million on that scale, you need take home only 6 cubic mms of sand, a bit less than 2mm x 2mm x1.5mm, or for those of you unfamiliar with the metric system, a cube 0.078 inches on each side. About as much sand as you can pinch between your thumb and forefinger. That's all. That's all you need to get your million dollars.

Simple.

What makes it even simpler is that the other kids in the sandbox are not paying attention. Luckily for you, they have no desire or intention to take even a single grain home with them. They are too preoccupied with other stuff, like leasing a BMW they can't afford. The sand is there for the taking. All you have to do is take it.

OK. How Do You Get It?

This, of course, is the million-dollar question. Quite literally.

There are lots of ways to get your hands on a million dollars, aside from stealing it.

First, you can marry for it.

If you Google "How to Find a Rich Man to Take Care of You," you get 4.8 billion hits. It's a pretty popular idea. Ironically, if you Google, How to Find a Rich Woman to Take Care of You, you get 1.4 billion hits. Something rather sexist in that. But add them up and you can find plenty of advice on how to marry for money. 6.2 billion websites devoted to this singular idea. You can see how popular the idea of having a million dollars is. Personally, I think this is not a very good plan, even if you could find a rich person to marry, which is pretty unlikely, what with so many other people trying this approach. However, I can tell you that everyone I have ever met who had actually done this has paid for it many times over. I don't recommend it.

Of course, you can be born into a wealthy family, but it's probably too late for that.

You can go on the TV show, *Who Wants to Be A Millionaire?* The show, not surprisingly with a title like that, is wildly popular. After all, who does not want to be a millionaire? There are over 100 international variations of the show. It is pretty much on the air somewhere any time you turn on a TV in any country on the planet.

You can try and win your million on *Who Wants to Be A Millionaire?* But the odds on this are slim. There have only been 6 people who have gotten all the way to a million dollars in the entire history of the American version of the show, out of nearly 4,000 episodes. So, this is probably not the best idea. The odds of winning a million dollars, long as they are on the TV show (and of course you have to be selected to be on the show in the first place) are in fact vastly better than the odds on winning a million dollars in a lottery, which are 1 in 11,688,054.

I can tell you for sure that one way you will not make you a millionaire, and that is by getting a good job and working very hard and saving as much as you can every month. This is a fast track to nowhere.

Let's assume you are earning $100,000 a year. As the median income in the US is now $66,000 a year, making a hundred grand is a pretty good number, and an aspiration for a lot of people. As it happens, 24% of Americans earn more than $100,000 a year. You might think you are doing pretty well if you're making a hundred grand a year. You are not, at least not if your goal is financial freedom. But let's see why.

Let's say you are living in Cleveland, Ohio, making $100,000 a year. We could make it San Francisco or New York, but come on, in Cleveland, that's a pretty good living, isn't it? Let's see. Of your $100,000 yearly income, you are going to pay $14,800 in Federal Income Tax. Then you are going to pay $2,800 in state income tax. Then you are going to pay $6,200 in Social Security Tax; $1,400 in Medicare and another $2,500 in Cleveland City Tax.

When all is said and done you are going to be left with $72,250 for the year, or $6,041.66 a month. Out of that $6,041.66 you are going to have to make your car payments, your mortgage, your food, clothing, cable, gas and electric, insurance, school fees, vacations and just about everything else. The Cost of Living Council estimates that the cost of supporting a family of 4 in Ohio will run you $73,570 a year, not counting child support, for which they add in another $14,489. That means you are going to maxing out your credit cards pretty much for the rest of your life, just to get by. But let's say, if you are really, really careful you might, might be able to sock away, let's say, $500 a month in savings. This is improbable, but let's say you are really disciplined. That means you are going to save $6,000 a year. So, it is only going to take you 166 years to save your first million dollars. If you started at the age of 21, you will be 187 years old when you hit the magic number. Just enough time, if you are really lucky and eat well and exercise daily, to get yourself that a really nice burial site.

So, there has to be a better way.

Fortunately, for you, there is.

And, you will be delighted to know, you have the power, and in fact, have always had the power to do this within you all the time. All you need to do is get in touch with it. That is what I am going to show you how to do.

RE-INVENT YOURSELF

I don't know if they do it in the Navy SEALS, but I know they do it in the US Army and at Parris Island for the Marines – basic training bootcamp. It's where they tear you down before they can build you up.

They tear you down so you don't cling to old ideas and old ways of thinking and acting that will be a detriment to your success as a Marine or a SEAL. They will tell you that your very survival is at stake and so it is critical that you divest yourself of old ways of thinking and acting and accept and absorb the lessons that the military is trying to teach you. It's for your own good. They make you into a different person.

I am going to do the same for you, and like Bootcamp, it is going to be difficult to let go of old ideas that you have been inculcated with since childhood, but if you want to succeed, it is essential. It is all those old ideas, ideas that you cling to, that are probably part of your very fabric and constitute a lot of how you live and see the world that are in fact, holding you back.

This may come as a surprise to you, but you already have the capacity within you to succeed, probably beyond your wildest dreams, you just don't know it. We all do. Let us call this your Human Capital. As you will discover, your Human Capital is the most powerful asset you own, yet most people spend their lives without ever engaging with it; without even ever being aware that it is there. It's a bit like having a super-power that you never use and never even knew that you possessed. But you do. You are, in fact, rather remarkably genetically engineered to succeed. But that drive to win has been beaten out of you. Like a wild horse, you have been broken so that you can be put in harness to drag someone else's plow around for the rest of your life so that they can make them their millions. We have to break you out of your harness and tap into your natural instinct to win, your Human Capital. It's already in your DNA, we just have to wake it up.

YOUR HUMAN CAPITAL

Life first appeared on earth some 3.7 billion years ago.

You are here today because you are the product of some 3.7 billion years of continuous evolution; a ruthless evolution in which only the strongest survived, generation after generation. Those first microscopic organisms are your great great grandparents, a billion times over. There is a direct line from them to you. Over and over again, for nearly 4 billion years, only those strongest organisms survived; those that had the will and the power to survive got to reproduce. You are the end product of an almost unbelievably long and difficult process of Darwinian elimination. You are here because you possess the genes not just for survival, but also for success against almost unimaginable odds. That power is within you right now.

For nearly all of those 3.7 billion years, the marker of who would survive and who would not was the ability to find food, and not to become food for someone else. Eat or be eaten. Eating was survival. If you did not eat you did not survive, and you were lunch for someone else. This was a constant fight, 24 hours a day, every day, every year for 3.7 billion years. This was pretty much the sole occupation of almost all of your ancestors. Only the very best and strongest lived long enough to create the next generation. You are the final product that that constant search for the best genes over an unbelievable 3.7 billion years. That is who you are. The best of the very best distilled down over and over for eons. You are not just a survivor; you are a winner. You have been genetically bred to win. It is modern society that has beaten that winning spirit out of you.

Today, and this is an extremely recent event in human history, the search is not so much the search for food, though it is derivative of it. The search is for money. Let us be brutally honest here. In the society in which we now live, there is a direct correlation between wealth and success. The search for food has been transmuted to the search for money. The more money you have, the more successful you are; the more successful you are, the more money you have. So, genetically, you are programmed to succeed; to be wealthy. You are. You already innately know how to make millions. The problem is that that knowledge has been consciously and purposely beaten out of you since your childhood. The way society is structured now, you are still in danger of being eaten – not physically, but rather spiritually. If you are an employee, if your life is now dedicated to makings someone else rich, then you are no longer the hunter- you are the food. I am going to make you the hunter. The power to be the hunter is still buried in there. We just have to re-kindle it. This is your Human Capital. We all have it. We have had is since we were born. It is in all of us. But it is lying dormant. Every effort has been made to kill it off. It's still in there though, like a glowing ember of an almost extinguished fire. We have to breathe life back into it, to re-kindle the flame.

YOU HAVE BEEN EDUCATED TO FAIL

If this is going to work, the most important lesson you are going to have to learn is to forget almost everything you know or you think you know about the world of work and money, and for that matter, how society and life are supposed to work. This may come as a shock to you, but You Have Been Educated to Fail.

That is, almost all of what you have learnt or what you have been taught has instructed and quite consciously trained you, by design in fact, to fail, or rather, not to succeed; to drop out of the competition, to eliminate yourself as a competitor. It is built into the system. Successful industry of any kind needs an army of hungry, frightened and obedient workers who will follow the rules; kept at their work-stations or cubicles by fear and anxiety. They and their labors are the food of the successful. The more obedient they are, the more deeply in debt they are, the more frightened they are, the harder they are going to work for you. It's actually a kind of slavery and it starts very early in life. You have a choice: eat or be eaten.

If you were like me, and it's a good bet you probably were, you went to public school, as did I. That was where you and I got our basic education, starting in first grade, and that is where the crushing of our Human Capital began.

Public education in America, and in the rest of the Western Europe, and indeed most of the world now, was actually a 19th century invention. It was the time of the Industrial Revolution. Factories and manufacturing were on the march, and the economy was booming both in the UK and in the US. The coming of the steam engine changed everything. Railroads moved goods across vast spaces for little cost, and steam driven factories manufactured vast volumes of goods at lower prices than ever before. Prior to the Industrial Revolution, it might take a woman, (they were mostly women), working at home, a week to weave a pair of stockings that she could then sell. This was the era of the cottage industry. Working at home with rudimentary tools, she and she alone spun the cotton into thread, then wove the thread into a singular item and then sold it. That was how she, and millions of others, supported their families. That was what provided them with an income. The arrival of factories with their spinning jennies and power looms meant that new machines could spin thread and weave it into hundreds of stockings an hour; later thousands and tens of thousands and a far lower cost. The cottage industries, and the families they supported, were driven to extinction.

The problem with factories, of course, is that you needed people to man them. This was deadening, mind numbing, stultifying work. Standing for 12 hours a day, feeding threads or raw cotton into a steam powered loom was a kind of living death, but also essential for the factory system to function. It was also incredibly dangerous. Often, children were employed, as their hands were small enough to reach between the running looms. Sometimes they were employed to crawl beneath the running looms to gather up bits that had dropped off. Limbs were often crushed. The air was filled with cotton dust that was easily combustible.

William Blake didn't refer to them as dark satanic mills for nothing.

But where were these people, these workers, to come from? They were going to come from the bucolic small towns, farms and villages; the people whose very livelihoods had been destroyed by those same factories. The young women who once wove a stocking a week were now needed to operate incredibly dangerous machines for twelve hours a day. The tranquil village life of colonial America or the English countryside was over. Now it would be factory workers living and working in cities, crowded into tenements, sometimes a dozen to a room; unspeakably unsanitary conditions, now rife with new diseases of the crowded industrial age.

But how could society be so quicky changed? How could former villagers or farmers be trained to accept the disciplines of factory work and life, not to mention its hardships? The answer was public education.

Public schools were not designed to teach you to think, they were designed to teach you to become a good and obedient factory worker; whether these were the cotton mills of Derbyshire, England, or the GM assembly line in Detroit, Michigan.

Think about what your own school experience was like. You were required to arrive at a certain time, let's say 9AM. If you were late, even by a minute, you were marked down, and you were in trouble. Just like in a factory. Then, a bell rang to start the day. Just like in a factory. An assembly line of "education". You stayed in a class for a prescribed period of time, say 45 minutes, at your desk, your work-station, doing your assigned task. Then, a bell rang, and you had 5 minutes to make it to your next work station (class) when the bell rang again. Those who were late were penalized. You got a 45-minute lunch break in the cafeteria, just like in a factory; then the bell rang again, and it was back to the assembly line (classes) until 3PM when the bell rang, and you were released from the factory (school) until the next day. You poured out of the gates and headed home, carrying your empty lunch pail, only to return the next day for more of the same. Just like in a factory.

You were allowed holidays off and a limited number of sick days, just like in the factory that you were being prepared for.

When it came to the actual work, you were trained from the first grade on to follow directions and do exactly as you were told, just like on an assembly line. Any deviation from repeating the same actions over and over was punished by a stern talking to, just like in a factory. If that did not work, your grade (pay scale) was reduced, just like in the factory you were being groomed for. If you were really recalcitrant, you were either held back (demoted) or worst-case scenario, expelled (fired). Those who did exceptionally well were rewarded with gold stars, a precursor to the Employee of the Month plaques that dominate factory walls and work-places.

Hour after hour, day after day, week after week, grinding year after year, from the age of 5 years old onward you were being taught to be a very good factory worker. Your Human Capital was slowly but surely ground down until there was not a whiff of a memory of it.

When it came to rewards, the very reason you worked so very hard, the more you adhered to instructions and manufactured (whether it was an essay or a multiple choice test), exactly what was expected of you, doing exactly what you were told to do, the higher your grade (the better your pay packet). Work hard, follow the rules and you will get the highest pay. The hierarchy of obedience was already deeply engrained in you.

If you did well you were promoted to the next level job (or grade), until finally, you graduated all ready to assume your spot on the assembly line, a process that you had been taught since the age of 5 and that you would continue to follow until you retired or died. You have never been educated to think or to question, you have been educated to be a good and obedient employee; a tool, a cog in the machine that makes wealth for others.

What the educational system beat out of you was any sense of independent thinking or action; and certainly, any thoughts of questioning the basis or validity of the entire system. These traits are the last thing you want in a good factory worker.

Now, you may say, that is all fine, but I don't work in a factory. I work in an office (even if you now do it virtually), it is a factory all the same. Rows of cubicles are no different from standing on the assembly line at GM or Ford. Your job is to manufacture whatever it is that the company for whom you work manufactures – even if it is banking or insurance or a law firm or accountancy. It's all factory work in the end and it all started when you were too young to know any better.

The 'system' does not honor your Human Capital. It does not honor your very DNA. In fact, it has no interest in it whatsoever, as any independent thinking merely serves to gum up the works. The factory system has nothing what-so-ever to do with who you actually are. This is the reason that, according to a recent Gallup Poll, 85% of people are dissatisfied with their jobs. And no wonder. The job has nothing to do with who you actually are.

You have been so very deeply conditioned to think and live in this way; it has been so woven into almost every aspect of your life that you no longer even think about it or think to even question it. It is just the way you work and the way you live, and the way, you believe, that the world is supposed to work, like your medieval ancestors. This disconnect between who we innately are and the kind of work we have been pre-conditioned to do is a cause of enormous stress. According to recent medical studies, a stress response that is not turned off, that pounds at you continually, is a major cause of anxiety, depression, heart disease and even cancer.

You know this is not good for you; you know something is wrong but you don't know what it is. You know you are not happy, but you also cannot see any alternative. After all, this is how the world is supposed to work – or at least that is what you have been pre-conditioned to believe.

This notion of 'how the world works', is a complete misnomer. The world works in the way that we want it to work; the way we, as individuals, decide it is going to work for us. If you were born 500 years ago, you would have, without resistance or a thought, accepted the idea that you were a land-bound serf, serving your Lord of the Manor who served the King. You would have spent almost all your time from a very early age working the land for someone else. You would have accepted this because you were condition to believe, and you did believe, that this was the way that God had ordinated the world. In a thousand years of the Dark Ages, there was never a serf who said, "hold on a second. Who put him in charge? I don't particularly want to live like this." Not one.

It is, indeed, the way the world works, but you actually don't have to be part of that world. You don't have to work your whole life to get your weekly pay packet. You want more, but to get it, the secret is not to work harder; which is what your employers would like you to believe. Work harder, Bob, and we'll increase your pay packet by another $100 a week. The secret, instead, is to completely break with the idea of 'this is how the world works,' and create the world that works for you. This is a process of re-invention and to get there, you are going to have to give up the myths and deep beliefs of what you are supposed to be doing. Freedom can be frightening, but it is well worth it in the end.

You will find that the most difficult part of getting in touch with your Human Capital and opening yourself up to a world of opportunity is going to be ridding yourself of very deep beliefs that have been carefully inculcated since you were five years old. But that is what we are going to do. That is the First Lesson.

PART III
9 STEPS TO SUCCESS

HOW DO YOU BREAK OUT?

My wife Lisa and I recently got a new puppy, an adorable rough coated Jack Russell terrier. Terriers are notoriously headstrong and willful, and perhaps as with all puppies, there were times when Murray would seem to lose contact with us and be lost in a world all his own – like when he would smell a rabbit or pick up the scent of another dog when we had him out for walks. When that happened, he would just take off, nose to the ground and all our yelling was for naught. He had lost contact with us.

The breeder from whom we bought the dog, and an excellent dog trainer, suggested filling a plastic bottle half-way with dried pasta. "When Murray locks in on something, shake the bottle vigorously, and the noise will startle him and break him out of his trance." It worked.

You are going to have to do the same thing. You are going to have to break yourself out of your trance. If you want to re-invent yourself, and free yourself from these very deeply believed dogmas (so to speak) which are so very destructive to you, you are going to have to shake up the pasta bottle a bit. Now, the sound of dried pasta being shaken is probably not going to snap you out of it, so we are going to have to try something else.

With Murray, we tried it and it work. The 'bang' of the pasta hitting the bottle snapped Murray out of his fixation on whatever it was that he was chasing and refocused him on us. You need, in a sense, to do the same thing. You need a 'bang' to snap you out of your complacency and allow you to focus on what is important – re-inventing yourself for a far better future.

Every rebirth, every renaissance, every 'born again' experience begins with a shock to the system. In the book of Exodus, Moses is an Egyptian prince who goes into exile in the desert but is transformed to a leader of his people by the shock of a burning bush talking to him. Michael Corleone is a prince of the Corleone family who goes into exile in Sicily and is transformed to the leader of his people by the shocking murder of his wife. Bruce Wayne is transformed to The Batman by witnessing the shocking murder of his parents. Luke Skywalker sees his aunt and uncle killed by stormtroopers and their farm set ablaze.

Call it Shock Therapy.

I said in the introduction that I had learned these 9 lessons over many years, and from some of the smartest people I have ever had the pleasure to know. And so, this was in fact the first step, the pasta bottle, and it was taught to me by one of the smartest people I have ever known, Professor Bob Gaudino. That man changed my life. He showed me lesson #1.

LESSON #1
SHOCK THERAPY

I grew up in a military family.

My father was a retired colonel in the US Army, but he ran our little household like it was basic training at Fort Dix. Admiral McRaven would have felt right at home in our house.

Saturday mornings, my father would stand at the bottom of the stairs and bellow up to us, "I'm coming up to inspect those rooms in 15 minutes and if they're not clean, no one is getting out of here. Do I make myself clear?"

He said, "There are three ways to do things – the right way, the wrong way and the army way." We did things the army way. So, I learned how to roll socks the army way, and to dress the army way. (You put on your button down pressed white shirt first, pull on your trousers, then open your trousers, fold down about 6 inches, grasp the shirt tails, pull back so the shirt is taught, then pull up the trousers and clasp so that the shirt remains board straight. Did you get that? Do it again.

Dressing like this, along with carrying my fiberglass briefcase to school pretty much guaranteed that I would remain dateless throughout high school. This gave me lots of time to study, so I was a very good student.

I was spending so much time studying, and not much else, that I got into one of the most competitive colleges in the country. Once I got there, along with my fiberglass briefcase, I continued to be the best, and loneliest student. Lots of time in the library. But I did get all A grades and I was, on the colonel's orders, on the path to Harvard Law, or Yale, at the worst.

In my sophomore year, I took a course in political philosophy from a professor named Robert Gaudino. We read Montesque and Hobbes and Kant and Diderot.

About halfway through the course, Prof. Gaudino asked me to stay behind. I could not imagine why. Perhaps he wanted to praise me for my excellent analysis of the Introduction to the Encyclopedia of Diderot by D'Alembert.

"Mr. Rosenblum," he said, as I waited to be showered with praise, "you are wasting your time here."

Needless to say, this was not what I expected to hear.

"You don't know who you are. You should drop out of the school."

It was not what I was expecting to hear, and my initial instinct was to ask, 'what in the world are you talking about?' But something deep inside me, perhaps a tiny voice said, 'here is the first person in the world who sees who you really are – or aren't perhaps would be a better word.' So, I listened.

He suggested that I drop out of school and spend a year experiencing the real world. It was, of course, a world I knew nothing about; the real world, that is. He would help me.

And so, working together, we found a family in Eastern Kentucky, in the heart of Appalachian coal country, that would take me in. He called these 'home- stays'. He called the whole thing 'experiential education'.

I would find local work.

Following Appalachia, I would go to Iowa, and he found a farm family where I could both live with them and work on their farm. That would be followed by a job on the Chrysler assembly line in Detroit, with a UAW family.

Needless to say, the colonel did not take well to this idea.

"Harvard law school is going to think you are out of your mind. And they would not be wrong," he bellowed.

Never-the-less, upon graduation in May, I loaded up my VW and headed down to Lick Branch Hollow, Kentucky, where I moved in with Liz and Bill Stacy and their family on Troublesome Creek.

On my way out the door, almost as an afterthought, I grabbed a little Kodak camera. It would come in handy for the next year. When people asked me what I was doing working in coal country, it was easier to say I was there to take pictures than to say, 'well, I am here looking for myself.'

From Kentucky, I went to Iowa to work on the farm, and after that, because the Chrysler plant was closed due to the oil crises, I got a job working on a construction site, first digging ditches and then pouring concrete for confinement breeders.

To say this was a life-changing experience would be a gross understatement. It was a complete and utter culture shock, but like the pasta bottle and Murray the puppy, it shook up my world. And that is what you need. You need something that is going to shake up your world in a way you could not imagine.

Like you, I was the product of an education from kindergarten onward, that was intended to break me and make me more pliable and more obedient. The foundation of that was the deeply inculcated belief that we all have, that I had to wait for permission before I could do something.

This belief, this need for permission, is deeply ingrained in all of us.

This is what school and work and society at large for that matter teach us day after day, hour after hour. It's endless and unrelenting. You may not cross the street until your parent gives you permission. You may not go into fourth grade until you have completed all the requirements of third grade. You may not get a promotion at work until your superior feels you have done all of your work to his or her standards; until you get a satisfactory performance review. We wait. You may not buy a house until you are given permission by the bank for a mortgage. It is endless. It is everywhere. We have created a society filled with red lights and stop signs, and we all have been trained to wait for someone else to give us permission to move on to the next level. This is what keeps us trapped for a lifetime.

If you are going to unwind so many years of subtle but unrelenting 'education', you are going to have to do something to break the pattern. You are going to need the 'bang' of the pasta bottle to snap you out of it.

One of my favorite books, and one I strongly recommend for you if you want to go on this journey is *The Hero with A Thousand Faces* by Joseph Campbell. The book is a study of 'heroes' throughout history, in literature, film, mythology and religion in every culture in the world, since the time of Homer and the ancient Greeks to Star Wars and the present. The journey of the hero is always the same, no matter what the story, no matter when in history: A person of little achievement or fame is suddenly called upon to carry out a mission. At first, they try and avoid it, but in the end, they pick up the challenge, go on a great journey, and with a few failures, ultimately succeed. This is the same story whether it is Moses in Exodus or Luke Skywalker in Star Wars and a thousand other heroes in between. This is the story of Muhammad, of The Buddha, or Joseph Smith, of anyone who has achieved 'enlightenment'.

The journey you are going to go on is, in many ways, no different. It is a very old human story, and one that resonates across the ages. The Israelites did not wander in the desert for forty years because they were lost. They wandered in the desert that long so that anyone with the memory of slavery would die off. A new generation had to be born that could enter the Promised Land, free of the memory being slaves. The is the notion of Re-Birth and Re-Invention. You don't have forty years to wait, so we have to do something else to free you of the memory of the shackles of your years being trained to be a good factory worker.

The first step is to break your connection with your past; with your perceived belief in who you are and how you are 'supposed' to behave – because that carries all the limitations that have been holding you back.

In my own case, I did just that thanks to Robert Gaudino who took me aside at the age of 19 and told me I was wasting my time at the school and wasting my life.

Nothing had prepared me for that bang of the pasta bottle. It was a shock to my system, and truly, it woke me up. It opened the door to the possibility of change.

Needless to say, when I came back to school, I came back a very different person. I had proven to myself that I could do what had appeared to be impossible things. Until then, my life had been very sheltered and circumscribed. The year away changed me in a fundamental way. I quit my pre-law courses and became a double major in history and studio art; and I picked up a camera and started taking pictures all the time.

In Campbell's book, the hero goes through a process of re-defining and re-inventing himself (they are almost all men). He does it by testing himself in a very hard task and proving to himself that he is capable of far more than he once thought. This is what I did, and what you must do as well. You must take yourself outside of your normal comfort zone and try and do something difficult; something really difficult.

Trust me, this works.

In Huxley's *Brave New World*, world dictator Mustapha Mond banishes Helmholtz to an island. Helmholtz chooses The Falklands. Mond cannot understand why, of all the islands, Helmholtz would choose The Falklands – cold, bleak and barren –

over some place like Hawaii. It is because, Helmholtz explains, we need something to fight against to feel truly alive.

It is the same for you. This is lesson #1. Pick something hard. Prove to yourself you can do it. This act will free you. It is, trust me, the first step to both your million dollars, but also to the freedom that comes with it. You need not go so far as to get a job in a coal mine, but you must pick something that is, to your mind, very hard and perhaps a bit frightening as well. In fact, the more frightening, the better. Perhaps sky diving? Take a karate class? Take a language class in Japanese. Pick up and learn an instrument. Something outside your comfort zone. Learn woodworking. Go take a weekend course in driving a racing car.

This notion of doing something even moderately hard, but certainly outside of your normal realm of comfort is important in two ways.

- First, it is going to give you the self-confidence, a belief in yourself, that you are capable of more than you might have thought previously
- Second, and I think perhaps even more important, it is going to begin to chip away at a crippling aspect of your life until now. Far too many of us live in a world that is in a sense provided for us. We all drive cars, but our relationship t the car is passive. Once, to drive a car you had to have at least a minimal understanding of how the car worked – you had to be able to change the spark plugs, to change the oil, to check the anti-freeze, to replace a fan belt and so on. Today, the only thing most people understand about their own cars is that they turn the key and it goes. We live, more and more, distanced from the actual functionality of our world – we are a bit like fish in a tropical fish tank. The water is oxygenated, the food appears, but we have no idea how or where it all comes from.
- Thus, this notion of challenging yourself to do something hard; something outside your comfort zone is an important

first step in freeing yourself from what we might call 'tropical fish tank world'.

Once you have succeeded in your challenge, whatever it is, whether it is skydiving or running a marathon, you will feel that you can now do anything. And it is true, you can. This is really the first step towards re-inventing yourself.

The next step is, as the chapter title suggests, to re-invent yourself. Once free of the burden of who society wanted you to be, you are now free to create yourself in an image that you like. This does not mean if you took a weekend course in learning to drive a race car that you are now on the path to being a racing car driver. What it does mean is that you are now on the path to being whatever it is you actually want to be, as opposed to being trapped in a life you think you are supposed to live.

YOU CAN BE WHATEVER YOU CAN IMAGINE

We are fortunate to live in an era in which you are free to become whatever you want to become; all you need do is do it. It is a freedom that we rarely, if ever, exercise.

For pretty much all of human history, we were, all of us, condemned to live the life our parents had lived, and the life our grandparents before them. We were, for almost all of human history, born into small, isolated villages and we died in the same village. Most people never traveled more than a few miles from the place they had been born. They married someone from their village. If your father was carpenter then you were a carpenter; if your father was a stone mason, then you would be a stone mason. Most people were serfs, spending their rather short and brutal lives working the land. If your father was a serf, then you were destined to be a serf. Your children would be serfs, and their children after them. This was the way of the world. This was, as any religion will tell you, the order of the world that God himself had ordained. You never questioned it. It was the way that world operated. It was the way the world was supposed to be. There was no other way. Of course, for women, the choices were far fewer, and most often simply none at all.

All that changed extremely recently, so recently in fact that the sense of a limited and rather circumscribed world is still deeply embedded within us.

Only in the last few years, perhaps only in the past 50 years or less, have opportunities that never existed before become open to everyone. I am old enough to remember when a woman going to law school or medical school made the newspapers. For most of American history, smart women had two options- they could become teachers, or they could become nurses. Now, with enough drive, they can become doctors, lawyers or CEOs of corporations. That is an incredibly recent change and one that is still not complete.

What is true for women is also true for everyone else. For the first time in human history, opportunities abound. But thousands of years of a closed and constricted society leave a deep psychological scar. This is what you must overcome, and it is not easy to do, but it is essential. The problem, as Paul Simon might write, is all inside your head, but so is the solution.

If you can prove to yourself that you can indeed do anything, the opportunity now is to completely re-invent yourself; and if you want to make your first million, this is the first thing you have to do. This is also very much in keeping with Campbell's view of the journey of the hero. The journey of the hero is really all about re-invention; re-inventing one's self. The metaphor for this notion of re-invention, of casting off the old and becoming something far more powerful is replete across almost every genre of literature and film. Walter White, frightened and failed high school chemistry teacher becomes the all-powerful and fearful Heisenberg. Peter Parker becomes Spiderman. Bruce Wayne, by donning his costume becomes the Batman. Mild mannered Clark Kent is transformed into Superman. The transformation of the weak to the strong; the loser to the successful. This is what you must now do. The transformation is entirely psychological, but it is the first and perhaps most important key to success.

There is a reason Hercules was faced with twelve labors. There is a reason Odysseus has to overcome a series of monumental challenges to make it home to Ithaca.

Once you start to see the world in this way, every successful person falls into the same pattern. Neo in The Matrix; NYPD Officer James Edwards in Men in Black; Katniss Everdeen in The Hunger Games; Harry Potter; Nemo; Mulan; the list is endless. Each of these characters undergoes a process of re-invention and re-definition of whom they are by facing difficult tasks. There is a reason pretty much every movie, every novel and even every religion is based on this concept – rebirth and re-invention. This is the first step to success, and it is the key to yours.

You are free to re-invent yourself as anything you wish, it is all within your grasp, but it should be something that you like to do; a persona you want to adopt; perhaps it is a model of a person you already admire; for you are now going to make your millions with this new identity.

My own advice here is that you re-invent yourself as something both interesting and creative. You don't have to re-invent yourself as a super-hero, but you since you are doing this you should re-invent yourself as something and someone you find interesting. You are going to be inhabiting this new person for a long time. You have the world to pick from. A writer; a musician; a dancer; a film-maker; an artist. You may, in fact, become anything you want to be. This is a moment of liberation. Take it. As Theodore Herzl wrote, "if you will it, it is no dream." For myself, at the age of 20, I declared myself to be a photographer. I had, in truth, never touched a camera before, but when I took off for Appalachia, I grabbed my father's old Kodak and a few rolls of film. The camera, I soon came to understand, gave me an excuse to be in places that I had never been before, and in all honesty, places that I felt extremely uncomfortable in. Being a photographer was a lot better as an identity and being a geek. Good enough for Peter Parker; good enough for Jimmy Olsen, good enough for me.

"What are you doing here?" the other coal miners would ask. Had I said I had come to 'find myself', or to 'look around', they would have thought me insane and probably never given me the time of day. But telling them I was a photographer gave me an excuse to being there and opened a door of access and accessibility; even if my pictures were terrible. It was an identity I put on like a costume, much the way Peter Parker becomes Spiderman, or Bruce Wayne dons his cape and cowl and becomes The Batman, and having donned it once, I never took it off.

Now, to be perfectly honest, I had very little talent as a photographer; and I still don't to this day. My pictures are mediocre at best. I have, over the years, had the privilege of working with some of the world's greatest and most talented photographer, and trust me, I was not then, nor would I ever be, one of them. But that made no difference when it came to freeing myself. I had assumed the identity and to start, that was all that mattered. I had succeeded in re-inventing myself; or at least I was certainly on the road to re-invention.

The thousand years of the Middle Ages, the Dark Ages, ended with the Renaissance. Renaissance literally means re-birth. For 1,000 years the western world had been locked into the Dark Ages – a brutal period of time. But with the Renaissance came the Enlightenment, the Intellectual and Scientific revolutions, the birth of art and literature – the world that we inhabit today. Re-birth. It is not for nothing that Fundamentalist Christians talk about being 'born again'. Re-birth. Re-invention. From that moment on, for the rest of my life, I would define myself as a photographer, and that made all the difference. It was something that was instantly recognizable to anyone. It was my own renaissance, my own re-birth, my own way of being born again.

Writer, musician, chef, dancer, clothing designer, photographer, influencer, film maker – go ahead, pick one. Who do you want to be? What do you want to be? Do it. Be bold. Take on the mantle. Become what you imagine in the best of your dreams. Here's a remarkable truth about our era – you may be anyone or anything you want to be, if you simply put your mind to it and embrace it. It is a unique time in history. You can do this.

LESSON #2
HIT THE ROAD

In pretty much every movie you have ever seen and pretty much every novel and every great story, the main character hits the road. That is, they head out of town on an adventure to somewhere. It is, in some ways, intrinsic to the idea of re-birth and re-invention. In the Homeric epic The Odyssey, Odysseus makes the long voyage from Troy back to his home in Ithaca but undergoes a change as a function of all of his adventures. This, of course, is re-invention. Religious pilgrimages such as the Haj for Muslims or walking the Camino de Santiago for Christians are all about the transformational journey. The Great Trek of the Afrikaaners, in South Africa; Mao's Long March; the Israelites in the Sinai. This is what Campbell refers to as 'the hero's journey'.

Odysseus heads back to Ithaca in The Odyssey. Luke Skywalker leaves Tatooine to learn the ways of the Force and become a Jedi knight. Mohammed leaves Medina to go to Mecca, then to Jerusalem on the Night Journey. In the Book of Exodus, not only Moses, but the entire Israelite people journey for 40 years across the Sinai. They did not wander in the desert for forty years because they were lost, they spent forty years to cleanse themselves of the memory of slavery and re-invent themselves as the Chosen People. Even in Miami Vice, Crockett and Tubbs are always jumping in a Ferrari or a Cigarette speed boat to go somewhere. The journey is paramount. In the best of these stories, the subject goes on a physical journey that also results in a spiritual or emotional journey; a transformational journey. There's a reason that so many epic stories have a journey as their center. It touches something very deep and very basic in our human DNA and in our deep history as a species. It connects, in a very fundamental way, to that Human Capital. Throughout history, many stories have no doubt been told, but the ones that we remember; the ones that we tell over and over again; the ones that have proven to mean something to us are stories that connect us to our Human Capital.

The more you look at stories that captivate us, the more you see the same repeating theme – transformation. The re-invention of the self as a new and far more powerful person. In Spiderman, Peter Parker is transformed to Spiderman. In Batman, Bruce Wayne is transformed to Batman. Mild Mannered Clark Kent steps into a phone booth and is transformed to Superman. Moses goes into exile in the desert and returns at the fearless leader of his people. Walter White, shy and retiring high school chemistry teacher is transformed into the terrifying Heisenberg. Re-invention of the individual to something more powerful and more successful.

Ironically, for most of our history as a species on this planet, we were nomadic wanderers. On a very basic level, that is who we still are at heart. Some 300,000 years ago, the earliest proto-humans were a tiny clan that began walking out of East Africa and went on to populate the planet. Moving; going places is deep in our DNA. That is why the notion of 'travel', of moving from one location to another is endemic to every great story in human history, and that movement, that odyssey, that trek, that pilgrimage transforms the individual. That is re-invention.

In Genesis 12:1, God instructs Abraham to leave his home and make a pilgrimage to a hitherto unknown place.

"And the Lord said to Abram: Go forth out of thy country, and from thy kindred, and out of thy father's house, and come into the land which I shall shew thee.

This notion of taking a trip and in doing so, re-inventing ourselves and our lives is very deep and very basic to us as human beings, and so is also intrinsic to our Human Capital.

When I graduated from college, I suppose I could have gotten 'back on track', as my mother might have said, and gone to law school. She even signed me up for an LSAT review course. But now going to law school was incongruous with my newly adopted identity as photographer. Instead, like everyone from Moses to Luke Skywalker, I hit the road.

I cannot tell you how both frightening and liberating physically leaving is. The whole point of travel is to get somewhere new, both physically and metaphorically. It is the very foundation of re-invention and renaissance which is actually Latin for re-birth. Born again.

In my own case, after I graduated from college, I spent three years traveling the world as a 'photographer'. I had received a fellowship from The Thomas Watson Foundation; a $6,000 stipend. It was enough to pay for some really good camera gear and a start to my travels. Now, I could never, in a million years have qualified for that grant as The Mothball I had started out as. But in my new persona, as the photographer who had gone to live in Appalachia, I was a good bet. Walter White became Heisenberg.

I was taking pictures for no one other than myself, but again, it gave me an excuse and an identity I liked. It helped me to grow into my new self.

In my first year, I went overland from London to Kathmandu, Nepal – relatively easy in those days. Many people were doing it. Then, like all young Jews, or many at least, I headed to Israel. Like them, I first wound up on a Kibbutz, but picking grapefruit in the hot sun was not for me. Instead, I grabbed an Egged bus, the national bus company, and made for Dahab. In those days, the Israelis were still in control of the Sinai, and Dahab was about halfway down the west coast, on the Red

Sea. It was little more than a Bedouin encampment, but it had, over time, also taken on the role of hippie destination, much like Goa, in India, but far less developed. Sun, sand, snorkel, sex and drugs. A perfect place to crash for a day, a week, a month or a year.

The local Bedouin had constructed some simple huts out of reeds. The place looked a lot like the set for Gilligan's Island. And so, I crashed there as well, along with about a hundred other similarly minded people from all over the world.

In the evenings, the inhabitants would gather around a campfire or two, sing songs, talk and occasionally get into political discussions. One night, I got into an argument with some guy who was there on R&R from the Peace Corps in Malawi. Our argument was over Palestinians. Well, as a Jew from New York, I knew the right response. "Israel must live. Holocaust. Palestinians were terrorists." I had all the answers. Then he turned to me.

"Your problem," he said, "is that you have never met a Palestinian in your life. You should go to Gaza."

Well, I thought, fair enough. I will go to Gaza.

This was, in fact, easier said than done. I took the bus back to Tel Aviv and headed right over to the main tourist office on Dizengoff Square.

"Can I help you?" the nice, blue-haired lady behind the desk said.

I smiled.

"Yes," I said. "I want to go to Gaza."

She stared at me long and hard.

"It's very dangerous," she told me. "You should go to a Kibbutz." And she handed me a stack of brochures.

"I have already been to a Kibbutz," I told her. "I want to go to Gaza."

Now her smile disappeared.

"You can't go there," she said in a very stern voice. "It's not possible."

Behind her was a large map of Israel with all the roads. There was Tel Aviv. There was Gaza. Clearly it was possible.

In any event, she was done with me. Looking over my head, she called to the backpack laden couple behind me.

"Next!"

Well, now a challenge. If I had been the same neurotic Jew from Long Island that I started as, I would have rushed back to the safety and the security of the Kibbutz. But that was no longer who I was. Now, I was, in my own mind at least if not yet in reality, an intrepid international photojournalist. I was on the journey of the hero. I had been presented with a challenge, and, as such, I would now have to rise to the challenge. Just as God had confronted Moses and challenged him with the burning bush, so too the old blue haired lady had challenged me. I would find a way to get to Gaza. As it turned out, you could take the Egged bus as far as Ashkelon, an Israeli industrial city on the coast, just a few miles from Gaza. So that is where I went. I would figure it out from there,

Checking into the Ashkelon youth hostel, I dumped my backpack and wandered around town. There was a large cement factory, and a lot of the workers were Palestinians. They commuted daily from Gaza to Ashkelon for work. I started to chat them up. Finally, one of them agreed to let me accompany him at the end of the next workday back to Gaza in a taxi. So, I went.

When the taxi got to the center of Gaza City, they dropped me off. Now, I was wandering around Gaza City on my own, not really knowing what to do or where to go. There were no youth hostels and no references to Gaza in my *Let's Go Israel* guidebook.

Finally, a car pulled up next to me.

"What are you doing here?" the drive asked me.

I explained that I as a photographer (again, the persona), and I had come to Gaza to take pictures.

"Hop in," he said, and he drove me to Marna House, the home of 80-year old Alia Shawwa, the doyen of one of the oldest families in Gaza. It was a large old house that stood atop a bluff looking out over the Mediterranean; a remnant of a much earlier time in the history of Palestine when the Ottomans and then the British ran the place and Gaza was a backwater for two Empires.

She invited me for tea, then to spend the night. The next day, she set me up with a family that lived in Beach Camp, one of the refugee camps that fill Gaza. I moved in for a month, taking pictures every day.

Was it frightening? Of course. Let's be honest here, The Mothball would never have wandered into Gaza. It was terrifying, but my newly adopted character, photojournalist, allowed me to overcome my fears. My belief that I was capable of doing such things allowed me the courage to go. And the funny thing is, the more stuff you do like that, the less fearful of life you become.

When I left Gaza after a month, I really felt I was ready now to spread my wings. I picked up some work as an archaeological photographer (it's all technical and not all that hard to do) on a dig in northern Israel, and having saved some money, headed off for North Africa. I landed in Tunisia and then crossed the Sahara Desert, making a left in Nigeria, through Cameroon into Zaire and onward to Sudan and Kenya; taking pictures all the way.

I traveled like that for three years. It didn't cost much. There were always odd jobs to find here and there. I cleaned toilets in the youth hostel in Jerusalem. I didn't care.

When I came back to the United States, much as I had gone back to Williams College after Iowa and Appalachia, I came back a very different person. Re-invented.

But now what to do?

Now, I am not suggesting that you pack up and head for Gaza or Afghanistan for that matter. But I am strongly suggesting that you take a pilgrimage, even a small one, in the guise of your new persona.

Think of it as a kind of test run. Get in your car or your truck and start to drive. Take a train or a bus to someplace you have never been before. Pick a destination – any destination will do. One of my students in one of my bootcamps engaged in what he called The Golden Pin. He would close his eyes and stick a pin in a map, and then head there to see what he could find – in search of a story, in search of an adventure.

The Nobel Prize winning physicist Richard Feynman is one of my personal heroes. Although he was a genius on a par with Einstein or Hawking, (he specialized in the integral formulate for quantum electromechanics), he was also eminently approachable to the averge person. He wrote a book that changed my life entitled, "*What Do You Care What Other People Think.*"

In 1970, he challenged his friend, math teacher Ralph Leighton, that the two of them should make a trip to Tannu Tuva. At first, Leighton thought Feynman, a noted prankster, was making it up, but as it turned out Tannu Tuva was a very small Soviet Republic, travel to which was almost impossible.

Feynman made it a lifelong goal to find a way to travel to Tannu Tuva. He and Leighton made up many excuses for how important it was for them to get to Tuva. Being Americans, in those cold war years, they were repeatedly denied. Tuva, Feynman once argued, was the home of the rapidly vanishing Tuva Throat Singers, but to no avail.

In 1991, Leighton wrote a book about the adventure entitled *Tuva or Bust*. In the book, Leighton explained that Feynman's never ending quest to travel to Tuva was an allegory to his never ending quest to explore new ideas and to push the boundaries of what had hitherto been considered impossible to achieve.

Feynman, who died in 1988, never got to Tuva, however his daughter Michelle finally made it in 2009.

So you must find your own personal Mecca, your Tuva, your pilgrimage to wherever and do it, for no other reason to prove you can.

LESSON #3 IT DOESN'T MATTER WHAT YOU DO, SO LONG AS YOU DO SOMETHING

A lot of people who want to make money agonize over what they should do. What kind of job should I get? What company should I work for? What qualifications should I have?

The best advice I can give you is, it doesn't matter.

If your goal is to get to your first million, it doesn't matter what kind of job you have or what you do. The world is so awash in money, there are so many opportunities, that if you keep focused on your final goal, the specifics of what company you work for or what kind of job you take do not matter a bit. What matters here is you. What matters here is the way you are going to see the world and attack it.

I self-identified as a photographer, and through that, not only found liberation from the past but also made millions in that persona. Ironically, I never, in fact sold a single photograph, but as it turned out, it didn't make any difference.

If you are dependent upon a company or a job to make your fortune, then it is all over. No one is going to do this for you, but you.

If, on the other hand, you are prepared to work with whatever opportunity comes your way and make it your own; if you are prepared to own your future and ask, (with a nod to JFK), not what can my job do for me, but rather, what can I do with my job, then we are ready to start.

In my own experience, which is really all I can write about, I started as close to the bottom of the barrel as you can get. But it all worked out fine.

I was certainly not going to go to law school now, not with my new identity as a world- traveling photojournalist, even if I had never got paid for a single photograph I ever took. Based on my now rather extensive travels and experiences, I was able to wrangle interviews with the photo editors of both Life Magazine, still in business then and National Geographic. However, once they saw my photos, they both agreed. "Nice," but no real talent there. "Thanks for coming by." Well, that was probably pretty accurate. But never let lack of innate talent stop you. In life, the rewards generally go to the most motivated, not the most talented.

At this point, however, it looked like I had at last reached the end of the road in my 'imaginary life', as my father called it. Now that I was home and had utterly failed in my delusional ideas, he said, it was time to buckle down and start to live in the real world – beginning, of course, with a real job. From an objective point of view, he might have seemed to be right. I was, after all, out of money and living on the couch in their one-bedroom apartment in Manhattan. From the outside, things looked pretty bleak, and to be completely honest, they looked pretty bleak from the inside too.

After a few months of this, my mother said that my father was willing to take me into the life insurance business, and that I should go downtown to his office and meet with him so I could get started.

This, in retrospect, was the sheer nadir of my life. The bleakest possible future awaited me. Changing your life is not easy and there are going to be a lot of ups and downs. The ups are fun. The downs can be devastating. So, after months of unemployment and a gnawing feeling that I had, in fact, been just kidding myself, I took the subway downtown to his office in one of the many grey and faceless buildings in the financial district, like a prisoner on his way to the gallows, with no seeming alternative but to die.

As luck would have it, when I arrived at his desk, I was told he was out to lunch. A small break in the clouds. I gathered my thoughts and headed out. A reprieve from my death sentence. The hand of God, or a tuna sandwich on rye with mayo, had clearly saved me.

But what to do now?

My mother, ever trying to be helpful had clipped a want ad (in the days before Craigslist) from the NY Times and handed it to me as I lay splayed across their living room sofa, my temporary home. "Daddy was very disappointed that you didn't want to work with him," she told me. "But here's a job," she said. I took the clipping from her hands, all of about 1-inch square, arose from the couch and called the number for Career Blazers.

"I got an interview tomorrow," I told my father.

"Finally," he said. "Be sure to dress well. Wear your good suit. He picked out one of his favorite paisley ties for me to wear as well. This was a big deal for him. He was very proud of his tie collection. "Don't get anything on it," he warned.

The next day, briefcase in hand, the same leather briefcase my father had given me for my 13th birthday; the same briefcase I had dragged through jr. high and high school (in case you were wondering why I could not get a date), I headed out for the Career Blazers offices in downtown Manhattan.

When I got there, I waited one of the molded red plastic chairs that were lined up against the wall until my name was called. I was then ushered to speak with a woman behind a grey metal desk. As we spoke, she filled out a form.

"Education?" she asked me.

I said I had graduated Cum Laude from Williams College.

"Community college?" she asked me.

“Small school in New England,” I told her.

She grunted and filled in a box.

“High school diploma?” She ticked the box.

“Can you touch type?”

“I had actually taken a touch-typing course in junior high. “60 words per minute,” I said. This was my first job interview, but even I thought it was a bit odd.

Then she rifled through a pile of papers.

“We have an opening at Merrill Lynch. Can you start tomorrow?”

Boy, I thought, I have hit the jackpot. I went home and told my father that I was going to be a stockbroker.

“Good career,” he said. “Merrill Lynch. Good company. What are the benefits?”

I told him I had no idea. He immediately grew annoyed. “What the hell kind of job interview did you have when you don’t even have the brains to ask what the benefits are when you are applying for a job.”

Fortunately, he didn’t ask what they were paying. I had forgotten to ask that as well.

The next day, in my best suit, my only suit in fact, still with the paisley tie, I headed downtown to the offices of Merrill Lynch on Broadway, clutching my empty leather briefcase. When I got to the reception desk, I told the receptionist I was here for my new job. She looked at me.

“Career Blazers,” I said.

She smiled. She picked up the phone and talked to someone, then told me to have a seat in the lobby. Someone would be down to meet me in a few minutes. And so, they were. A middle-aged woman in a blue dress came down, introduced herself, shook my hand and bade I follow her into the elevator, which silently whisked us up to the eleventh floor. From there, she guided me down a long hall to a large conference room.

The room was empty but there was coffee and cookies at the far end.

"Help yourself," she said.

I thought that we were first in for the meeting, and probably the partners would come soon to meet with the new soon to be stockbroker. There were piles of papers on the conference table. Messy, I thought.

"Have you ever alphabetized anything?" she said to me.

I said I had not.

"Well," she said, "it's pretty easy. Start by making three piles, A-H, I-P and Q-Z." And she left.

That was the job. Get these thousands of pieces of paper in alphabetical order.

Career Blazers, as it turned out, was a temp agency. I was a temp at Merrill Lynch. After two weeks alphabetizing at Merrill Lynch, I would be sent to a bank, then an insurance company, then a law firm. Alphabetizing, answering phones or typing. My father had been right. I was a loser.

Then, one day, they sent me to a TV station. I had absolutely no knowledge of television, except for watching it. It was a TV newsroom. ABC News, to be precise. And the job was to sit at a typewriter and transcribe interviews. $10 an hour, which was pretty good in those days.

The job was pretty monotonous and pretty predictable. A tape of the transcripts of a bunch of interviews; a foot pedal to pause the tape, and an IBM Selectric typewriter. Sit and listen and type. No one talked to you. You were on your own.

Then, about a week or so into the job, everything suddenly changed in an instant. One morning, all hell broke out in the newsroom. People were running around like maniacs. The phones were ringing. Papers were flying and people were yelling at each other.

I took off my headset and turned to the guy next to me, another typist.

"What's going on?" I asked.

"The Iranians just seized our embassy in Teheran," he told me.

Well, that was interesting, but not my problem. I resumed my typing.

Suddenly, some older guy burst into the newsroom and raised his hands. Everyone fell silent.

This was George Merliss, who was the Executive Producer for Good Morning America, the show for which I had been typing transcripts.

Like General Patton at the Battle of the Bulge, Merliss began to call out orders.

"You," he said, pointing at some producer. "Call the White House." Then he spun 30 degrees to his right. "You!" he said, "call the Pentagon!"

Everyone in the room got an order. Then his finger fell on me. I am sure he had no idea who I was or what I did, but it was all hands to the pump.

"You!" he said, pointing at me, "call the Islamic Center in Washington."

Well, $10 an hour is $10 an hour. So, I took off my headset and picked up a phone.

Someone answered.

“Salaam Aleikum,” I said. “Ana min al- Good Morning America...”

That was as far as I got. I felt a hand grip the collar of my shirt and pull it upwards.

“You speak Arabic??”

It was Merliss.

“I do,” I said. Well, I had picked up some in my years of travel. Enough to order a coffee. Enough to make out a headline in a newspaper. Enough to quote a few lines from the Koran.

“Where did you learn?” Merliss ordered.

Now, here is one of those moments of opportunity when the door opens a crack. The trick is to go in. You can worry about the details later.

“When I lived in Iran,” I said.

This was, on the face of it, ridiculous. First, no one in Iran speaks Arabic, they speak Farsi. But, needless to say, no one in Good Morning America, or probably all of ABC News for that matter, knew that. As for having lived in Iran, well, I had been to Iran, and I had been alive, so I thought that was more or less true.

“Do you know anything about these hostages?” he asked me.

“Sure,” I said. Which was true. I knew there were hostages and I knew they were in Iran. The guy at the next desk had told me.

Merliss spun around and pointed at one of his people. “Get this guy a desk and a typewriter!” He failed to notice that I already had both. But in that instant, I was removed from the typing pool and made a Middle East Expert for the Iran Crisis.

I cannot emphasize this enough. When the door of opportunity opens, even a small crack, jump in with both feet. There is no upside to holding back. Go for broke. You have nothing to lose and everything to gain. Just go for whatever opportunity presents itself. You'll figure it out later. Everyone else does.

A bit later that day, we were all called down to a massive conference room deep in the bowels of ABC Network News. The room was packed with producers, Executive Producers and a few reporters and even anchors whose faces I knew, of course, from TV.

The room grew silent as a woman named Phyllis McGrady, a Vice President of ABC News, so I was told, took center stage at the front of the room. She began to lay out ABC News' approach to covering the now just breaking Hostage Crisis. And with that, she pulled down a world map and took about 10 minutes to find Iran. This job was going to be a piece of cake.

Soon, I was briefing one of the two hosts of the show, David Hartmann, who before Good Morning America, had been a TV doctor on a show called Lucas Tanner, MD. He was about as qualified to be a journalist as he was to be a TV doctor, so we were a good fit. I quickly found that if I read the NY Times and the Wall Street Journal before I came to work, I would be about the best-informed person in the room. My duties soon extended beyond Iran. On the anniversary of the Battle of Stalingrad, I was to brief Hartmann on Josef Stalin. He was confused. He was our ally in the Second World War, but he was also, apparently, a mass murderer.

"I don't understand," Hartmann asked me, perplexed, "so was Stalin a good guy or a bad guy..." That's American TV news for you.

I had, entirely out of whole cloth, spun myself from being the typing temp to being the Middle East expert for ABC News. That, my friend, is re-invention.

The Iranian Hostage Crisis went on for an astonishing 444 days. Alas, Good Morning America's interest did not last that long, and at some point, I found myself out of a job. I suppose I could have gone back to Career Blazers, or gone to law school for that matter, but working in the TV newsroom I thought, this looks like an interesting career.

I had spent enough time at Good Morning America to see that a) television news was not exactly filled with the smartest people in the world, and b) there was a lot of money sloshing around there and the work was a whole lot easier than, say, being a corporate lawyer. As it happens, there is a lot of money sloshing around in every business. The trick is not to become an employee, but rather to affiliate yourself with some industry or business through which all that money sloshes. It doesn't have to be television, though that worked for me. It can be any business – fashion, food, travel – you name it. Like picking up the mantle of your new identity, use that new identity to slide into a business that later be mined for millions and you're on your way.

I got into the television business. Well, it was close to photography, sort of, wasn't it, even if I had never taken a decent picture in my life. I landed myself a job as a Production Secretary at WNET/13, the public television station for New York. But in my case, my job with a show called Mainstream. This was about as close to starting at the bottom of the TV world as you can get, but as Richard Feynman says, there's plenty of room at the bottom.

Mainstream was a half-hour public affairs program about events in New Jersey, consisting of a host, Tom O'Neill, who was some kind of local New Jersey politician, but had learned to an outstanding imitation of a corpse when he was on air. He was the antithesis of what we would call live. He was joined each week by a guest sitting in swivel chairs on a set made up of the New Jersey state flag and a potted palm tree. It aired once a week, on Saturday mornings at 6:30 AM. I could not even convince my mother to watch it.

My job, as Production Secretary, was to slice the bagels and make the coffee for our host and guest. I got paid $300 a week, which was enough to rent a third story walk up in what was then the far less than fashionable and somewhat dangerous Brooklyn. I was a million miles from my first million dollars, but at least on the path to it, even if I did not realize it at the time.

This is the kind of job where you can either kill yourself or you can say, well, there's something here, somewhere, if only I can find it. I was, after all, in the 'television business', very broadly speaking, and that was enough.

The great thing about having such a crap job was that no one really cared what you did, as no one was watching, either you or the show. This turned out to be great news. Also exiled in this Newark gulag was a science show called Innovation. I think it aired after Mainstream. It was supposed to feature cutting edge science in New Jersey. Go ahead, make your own jokes.

In the run-up to the 1984 Presidential election in the US, there were 3 candidates vying for the spot – Walter Mondale, Gary Hart and Jesse Jackson. As part of its public service duties, WNET/13 had decided to run an 'Election Special' during the Democratic primary in New York. This was a big deal for WNET/13, and they had gotten all 3 candidates to agree to appear live from the New York studios.

But as this was an unusual event for WNET/13, there was no regular staff to manage it. One afternoon, a sign was posted in the hall. Anyone interested in working on the Election Special, it said, should come to a meeting next Tuesday in room 144 in the New York studios. Peggy Girshman, a producer at the Newark science show, Innovation, told me I should come to the meeting. She was going. So, I went.

There were about 100 people in the room. Someone at the front of the room was yelling out jobs to be filled.

"We are looking for segment producers," the meeting leader yelled.

“Put up your hand,” Peggy said. I liked her so I did.

In a moment, I had been selected to be a segment producer for the Election Special.

“Have you ever produced anything before?” some executive asked me.

“Sure,” I said. I had produced bagels and coffee. So here is a good piece of advice. Even if you don’t know how to do something, go for it anyway. I mean, aside from brain surgery, how hard can it be? If other people can do it, so can you. This little piece of advice has made me a fortune over time.

My father used to say to me (and not in the nicest way, “if you could learn to package bullshit you would be a millionaire.” It was, in fact, the best advice the old man ever gave me.

I was told to proceed to the field shop in the basement and meet with the camera crew that I would take with me to Jesse Jackson headquarters at the Hilton Hotel on 6th Avenue and 53rd Street. I was told to produce a 3-minute report on the Jackson campaign that would run that evening with the live program. As each candidate was introduced, the 3-minute ‘packages’ would air. Any half-way producer in the TV news business would be able to do this with their eyes closed. Alas, as my only experience in actually making television was limited to slicing bagels for people who were going to be on television, I was at something of a disadvantage. However, never let lack of experience, or knowledge for that matter, hold you back. There is only one way to learn and that is just go all in and take your shot.

I had absolutely no idea of what I was doing, but I headed down to the field shop and met with Dale Vennes, the camera guy and Nick Pavicavich, who ran audio. They had been with WNET/13 for years. We loaded the gear into their van and headed off to the Hilton.

As soon as we got there, it must have been obvious to Dale and Nick that I did not have the vaguest idea of what I was doing. They could, I suppose, have helped me out. Instead, they decided to have some fun.

"What lens would you like, Mister Producer?" they asked.

I had no idea. "The normal one," I said.

"What kind of shots would you like here Mister Producer?" they asked.

"The regular ones."

Unfortunately, they did exactly what I told them to do.

Worried that I would miss something, I had them shoot everything I could think of, and so, already late, I ran back to the Channel 13 studios with a pile of tapes, checking my watch. I was assigned to an edit suite on the 4th floor and there met Freddy Rodriguez, who would be my editor.

Now, Freddy was a very nice guy and he could see right away that I had absolutely no idea what I was doing. But it was already 4PM and the Election Special was scheduled to start at 5PM, live.

Freddy said, as any good editor would say, "what do you want to do now?" So I just made stuff up. If I had come in with a mess, I was busy making a mess into a major disaster.

"Put that it," I said. "Now that shot. Now that one..."

Freddy would turn to me.

"Are you sure?"

I was pressured. "Just do it."

What Jackson Pollack was to painting, my video was to television.

Soon the phone started to ring. It was Joan Konner, the Vice President of Channel 13. "Where is the Jackson piece?" she yelled.

"It's coming!" I said.

More mess. Then more.

Finally, the disaster was done.

Freddy popped out the tape and handed it to me.

"Good luck, man," he said as I ran out the door.

It was now 5:20. We were 20 minutes into the live show. They had already aired the Walter Mondale profile and the Gary Hart profile. Only Jesse was missing his bit.

Just like in the movie Broadcast News, I ran down to the control room for the big master studio for WNET/13, clutching the finished piece in my hand. The room was filled with every executive and every big wig from New York public television. Joan Konner was sitting in the big Captain Kirk director's chair running the live show.

I handed her the tape. The show was nearly half over by now.

"About time!" she said, then put it into a playback deck to take a look at it before she let it go out to air.

My story probably ran about 3 minutes. 45 seconds into her screening, she hit the eject button, took the tape out, stood up and threw it as hard as she could against the glass wall that separated the control room for the studio. The resounding crash silenced the entire room.

"This is shit" she yelled to me and everyone in the room. Then she pointed at the door. "Get out!" she screamed. "You'll never work in this industry again!"

I made it back to my job cutting bagels and making coffee in Newark, once again contemplating law school.

Three months later, Fort Dix in New Jersey was closing. WNET/13 decided they wanted to do a special on the closing of the army base. Anyone who was interested in working on it was invited to a meeting in room 144 in the New York headquarters of the network. Of course, I went. There were about 100 people there.

When they asked who wanted to work on the series as a producer, I put up my hand.

"Have you ever produced anything before?" they asked me.

"Sure," I said, "during the election."

"OK. Well get down to the field shop and pick up the crew."

This was on a Friday afternoon. The shoot was scheduled for the following Monday morning. *A Soldier's Story,* the Denzel Washington break-out movie had just been released. Well, it was about the army and soldiers so I thought I would go and see it. In fact, I watched it twelve times over that weekend, and I took copious notes on how it was made; what it looked like, shot by shot. Close-up on the flag, wide shot of people marching, close up on the boots, close up on the soldier's faces...

On Monday morning, I appeared at the field shop, and there were Dale and Nick, waiting for me.

"Oh, Mister Producer," they said, "still got a job? Where are we going today Mister Producer?"

When we got to Fort Dix, they asked me, "what kind of shot do you want here, Mister Producer?"

This time, I had an answer. "Close-up on the flag, wide shot of people marching, close up on the boots, close up on the soldier's faces..."

When I got to the edit, there was Freddy Rodriguez.

"Hey man, you still got a job here?" he said.

I told Freddy how to lay in the shots. I just reproduced what I had seen in the movie. Close up on the flag, close up on the faces, wide shot. Like in the movie, I laid in a soundtrack – in this case, America, the Beautiful by Ray Charles.

"Hey man," Freddy said, "You have gotten really good at this!"

When the piece aired, people cried. I got a call from Joan Konner. I was no longer a production secretary. I was now a producer.

You see, how hard was that?

What is the take-away here for you, the aspiring millionaire? In our world today, there are almost no secrets. Everything is right in front of you, and most of them follow a pretty predictable formula.

You want to be a great filmmaker? Just turn on Netflix, but watch it as a YouTube instructional video, not as a movie. The best filmmakers in the world are there showing you how to do it. Learn from them.

You want to be in the fashion business? Take a look at what is selling and copy it. If it works for them, it will work for you.

Picasso said, "good artists copy, great artists steal," so steal away. Every successful person in the world steals. The first personal computer, at least as we know it today, was not invented by Steve Jobs or by Bill Gates. It was, instead, invented by Xerox PARC (Palo Alto Research Center). It had most of the features you would recognize today – a graphical user interface that was in black and white and looked like yours looks, a mouse and a cursor – these in a day when computer screens were all green flashing lights and codes. It was called the Xerox Alto. The Alto also had email, word processing and a calendar.

But Xerox had no interest in the Alto. They were in the copying machine business.

In 1979, Steve Jobs visited Xerox PARC and saw the future, and copied it. It put Apple years ahead of his nearest competitor, Microsoft. Years later, Bill Gates commented: *"I think it's more like we both had this rich neighbor named Xerox and I broke into his house to steal the TV set and found out that you had already stolen it."*

So by all means, steal away.

A friend of mine is a great fan of NLP, Neuro-Linguistic Programming. One of the foundations of NLP, so he tells me, is something called Modeling. In Modeling you observe the behaviour of someone you admire, or the structure of a business you admire, and you copy it. I am not sure about NLP, but I am sure that this works. So, Model or learn from the best by watching what they do and repeat it.

As a producer at Channel 13, I was paid marginally better, but not much. Let's remember this was still Public Television. But at least I was making stuff. I won a few Emmys, but who does not, frankly. And I had the formula down on how to make TV. It's a lot like baking cookies. Just follow the recipe over and over and it will come out fine. As with most things in life, once you understand the repeatable formula, you can become quite good at anything.

A few years ago, Malcom Gladwell wrote a very popular book called *Outliners.* One of the basic, and perhaps best-known theses in the book was that if you do anything for 10,000 hours, you can be a world-class expert. Practice the piano for 10,000 hours and you can become an accomplished pianist. Play chess for 10,000 hours and you can become world-class chess player. Play tennis for 10,000 hours and you can be as good as any country club pro. That is because as homo sapiens, we are capable of learning pretty much anything, and most things in life, whether it is chess or tennis have a repeatable pattern to them.

These patterns are all around us, and thanks to the Internet and YouTube, among other things, the patterns are all there for you to observe and learn from. Making TV or movies, it turned out, as no different. Learn the pattern and simply repeat it.

Learning to see and replicate patterns is a very important step on your road to your first million dollars. The answers are, in fact, not only all around you, but actually right before your eyes, all you need do is look, or rather, observe.

That's what I did in the TV business. I watched as much as I could, I took notes, and pretty soon I came to see, that like everything else in life, there was a repeatable formula for success. Learn the formula, repeat it and you are well on your way.

After a few years, and a few awards, I got hired by the big network, CBS News, as a producer for one of their flagship shows, Sunday Morning.

Now, as a producer for CBS News, I was making $100,000 a year. I moved to a much better apartment on Central Park South. But trust me, this is actually not much closer to the first million than was the job at PBS. A salaried employee is still a salaried employee.

And even though I was making more money and now was working for a respectable TV show that a lot of people watched and had a better apartment, it was still, after a while, the same old factory work.

One day I looked down the hall and saw one of my fellow producers. He was in his 60's and had been there for years. I was making $100K, he was making $140K, and there I saw my future. He did pretty much exactly what I did, day after day, week after week, year after year.

So, I quit.

After so much work to re-invent myself, to create a new persona, I found myself caught in the same trap – factory work for a salary. No matter how hard I worked I was never going to make my first million like this, not unless I became the President of CBS News, and that was statistically very very unlikely. No, this was not a pathway to millions. Jobs never are.

LESSON #4
GO ALL IN

If you are going to re-invent yourself and make your first million, you have to be 150% committed; almost blindly committed to your own success. Half-way measures are not going to work.

Well, of course my friends and family all thought I was out of my mind.

"You are walking away from a great job!" they all said.

"What are you going to do now?"

Well, I wasn't too sure, to tell you the truth. I just knew that working in a factory, even a TV factory, was deadening. It was no different, in many ways, from working on the assembly line at Chrysler or GM or Ford, but instead of making cars, we were making TV stuff. No different in the long run.

I found the entire process of making television frustrating. It had been fun in the beginning, but once I learned the formula, and it is, like pretty much everything else in life, very very formulaic, it quickly became boring. Also, I had been used to working on my own, traveling around the world taking pictures, going where I wanted to go and spending time with the families that I lived with before I photographed them. At WNET/13 in Newark, they also left me alone, mostly because no one ever watched the show. But at CBS, every decision required a meeting and an endless discussion, and the TV was made by a team with camera people, sound people, directors, producers, editors, senior producers, senior executive producers, executive producers. It was endless. I was just a cog in a wheel, not different from a million other jobs in the corporate world.

So, in a moment of arrogance, stupidity and probably a kind of insanity, I quit.

I thought, "I can make TV news by myself. I don't need CBS News."

Now that was at that moment, inherently crazy, but it is also the seeds of personal re-invention. You have to have the courage to break out on your own and try something crazy. Maybe it's starting a food truck. Maybe it's creating your own cosmetics line in your kitchen. Maybe it's making your own clothing line in your bedroom. It doesn't matter what the 'thing' is, but that moment when you break away and say, I am going to take a shot now and I am going to do it myself, to me is the defining step on the road to your first million.

Many years after I left CBS, when I was out funding one of my companies, one of my first investors was a man named Alan Sidnam. Alan was then the Vice Chairman of Ogilvy-Mather, the worldwide advertising agency. He put money into one of my ideas, but he also gave me a great piece of advice that I am passing on to you.

He said, if you're going to do something, you have to have the courage to **go all in**. "Guys who go to Vegas and put one chip down on a number in roulette may win," he said, "but they are never going to win big. If you want to win big, you have to have the courage to go all in. Put all the chips on one number you believe in and see if it hits."

So that is what I did at CBS News. I went all in. I quit, I bought myself a small hand-held video camera because I could not afford a professional rig and I headed out to try and make TV news by myself.

I knew I would only get one shot, and I knew that if I took my video camera and started shooting in New York no one would notice. I needed a home run at my first and only time at bat. So, I got on a plane and I headed for...where else? Gaza.

It was the height of the first Intifada, the Palestinian uprising against Israeli rule in the Occupied Territories, and there was no place hotter than Gaza. I went back to Marna House, and Mrs. Shawa took me in. She kept me there for a week, questioning me all the time about what I wanted to do. As I said, tensions were high and my presence there did not go unnoticed.

Finally, after a week she turned to me.

“Rosenblum,” she said, “you’re a Jew, but I trust you.”

And so, with her sanction, I was taken to a home in the Jabalya Refugee Camp, and as was my style, I moved in with a family for a month, shooting video every day,

The Intifada was, of course, being covered by every network news organization in the world. But almost all of them stayed in Tel Aviv and would arrive each morning at the Erez Checkpoint, the border between Israel and Gaza and there the reporters would line up to do their live feeds and stand ups, accompanied by Israeli film crews and by the Israeli army to protect them.

My take was different. I was inside. And I lived there. I got access none of them could get. When there were shootings and injuries, the ambulance taking the wounded to Shiffa Hospital would stop to pick me up. That kind of access. I also focused less on making TV news pieces and more on making a small movie- a character, an arc of story and a resolution. People love movies, they pay to go to the movies. No one pays to watch the news. Movies beat news every day- so make news like it’s a movie.

After a month of living and filming in Gaza, I was pretty much out of money and it was time to go home. To what, I was not sure.

I had quit a top job at a top TV network on what seemed like a crazy whim and what increasingly looked like a stupid idea. Now all I had was a pile of tapes. No job, no career and no prospects. Not knowing what else to do, I took my pile of tapes to see Les Crystal, the Executive Producer of what was then called The McNeil/Lehrer Newshour and today is the PBS Newshour. I didn't know Les Crystal, but I wrote him a letter explaining my story (this is going to prove seminal for you soon), and he agreed to meet with me.

When he saw what I had shot, he bought two stories from me for $50,000.

No employee of CBS News could have ever dreamt of being paid $50,000 for two stories. It was as far from their realm of reality as our medieval peasant starting his own clothing line. Neither could The Mothball of Williams College have been paid that. But the persona that I had invented, the world-traveling fearless filmmaker could and did.

Now, as it turned out, that was pretty good for one month's work. But it was also a deal for Les Crystal. If he had sent a team – a reporter, a producer, a camera crew to Gaza for a few days, let alone a month, it would have cost him far more just in air fares, hotels, meals, rental cars, fixers, translators and security.

"What else have you got?" he asked me.

So, I got on a plane for Cambodia and headed north to where the Communist insurgent Khmer Rouge held half the country. Like I said, all in. Following that, I spent three months in Uganda finding the Index Case for AIDS for Ted Kopple and the ABC News show Nightline.

OK, still not a million dollars in sight, but I had really done a great job in re-inventing myself, and trust me, that is the key. No one invests in someone who is a really good and obedient employee, no matter how great their quarterly performance reviews are. You have to **re-invent yourself**, then **hit the road** and **go all in** so you can stand out from the crowd. You might call this building your brand. **Do not be afraid!**

Are you getting the concept here?

The world is filled with people who are 'good workers.' It is not worth, as John Nance Garner once said of the Vice Presidency, a pitcher of warm spit – or some other bodily fluid. Have the courage to become something different, something interesting and then do it, even just a bit, and the people will start to throw money at you. Money, as I came to learn, does not invest I ideas, it invests in people. It seeks out interesting, creative people who have the courage to take a risk, even if it doesn't always work out the first time, or the second or third for that matter. The trick is to just close your eyes and do something, and if it doesn't work, do it again until it does. And it will.

In my case, the guy who beat a path to my door was a Swedish billionaire named Jan Stenbeck. At some dinner part, I met the next-door neighbor of a friend. The neighbor was named Mike Tannen and he was a lawyer for Stenbeck. Casually, Tannen asked me what I did for a living. I told him, I traveled around the world on my own making TV news stories with a small hand-held camera. Now, that is an interesting story. He said he wanted me to meet Stenbeck.

Stenbeck, who had made his fortune in mining and forestry was now busy building the first commercial TV networks in Sweden. Until then, Sweden only had one channel SVT, the Swedish state broadcaster. He was going to shake up the media world of Sweden, or at least he was going to try. All in.

When I met Stenbeck, I explained what I had been doing, and then, he asked me the seminal question that would shape the path for the rest of my life. Stenbeck immediately understood the financial implications of what I had done. I had, in a stroke, gotten rid of the camera person, the sound person, the producer and the editor. He turned to me and said, "can you teach other people to do this?"

I replied in an instant.

"Any idiot can do this."

Trust me, no good employee of a TV networks ever talked like that, and neither did The Mothball, but those days were behind me now.

We continued chatting. Then, there was a moment of silence. He seemed to be thinking.

"Tell me again what it is that you do," he said.

"I travel around the world making my own TV news stories," I told him.

He glared at me. He was a very big man and he could be very scary sometimes.

"No!" he thundered. "You are the world expert in the television news revolution."

Here, I could only smile.

"I don't think so," I said.

This really seemed to piss him off.

"You are the world expert in the television revolution. From now on, if anyone asks you, that is what you tell them. Let other people say you are not. But that is who you are."

To me, it sounded ridiculous. Ridiculous and arrogant for that matter. But who am I to argue with a self- made billionaire? So, from then on, I was the world expert in the television revolution. I kept saying it all the time to anyone who would ask, and often to people who did not even bother to ask. And it was true, in the beginning, it did sound ridiculous. But if you say it long enough, that is what you become, both in other people's eyes, and in a weird way, in your own. Only later did I come to realize that this was but another step in this process of re-inventing yourself; of creating an entirely new you.

LESSON #5 DECLARE YOURSELF TO BE THE WORLD EXPERT.

This may seem, on the face of it, to be a completely insane, not to mention incredibly arrogant thing to do. But, Stenbeck did not become a self-made billionaire for nothing. What he told me actually works. And this is the critical step in personal re-invention.

And I can tell you from personal experience, people are willing to pay a lot to work with the world expert in the television revolution, or anything else for that matter. As there is no official Board of Certification for World Expertise, if you declare yourself one, well, why not?

This was the definitive moment of self-re-invention. If you're going to re-invent yourself, you may as well go for broke. Aim for the stars. There is, in fact, no one to stop you but yourself.

I am reminded here of the wise words of the sage Hillel the Elder, (80 BC), who said, "If I am not for me, who will be?"

He also added, "If I am only for myself, then what am I? And, if not now, when?" The guy could have been a management guru in a later age.

So, go be for yourself, as no one else will be. Declare yourself the world expert in whatever field you have chosen, in whatever persona you have decided to re-invent yourself as. As Jan Stenbeck said, "let other people say you are not."

If you are a baker go ahead and declare yourself the world's greatest cake maker. I have a neighbor who makes the most amazing scones I have ever eaten. She could easily and properly declare herself world's greatest scone maker, or her product world's greatest scones. Who is going to argue? And if they did, is there a board of scone certification that they could appeal to? I think not.

Now, here is the point in all of this. People will pay a lot more to deal with the world's greatest expert in whatever field you have than they will to deal with some schmeggie down the street. More interestingly, and perhaps more importantly, calling yourself 'world's best' or 'world expert' elevates you in your own eyes in a strange way. It is part of the never-ending process of renaissance, of re-birth; of re-invention. If you are the world's best then you try and live up to that every day, and every day you try and make yourself even better.

World's Best or World Expert is how you are going to define yourself from now on. And why not? That is who you are.

When I Google "world expert..." the first thing that comes up in the search window is "World expert in bread baking, as I like bread, I get someone named Richard Bertinet as my first hit. Have I ever heard of Richard Bertinet? Never. I go to his website and he declares himself "bread genius." He also offers courses in bread making, online, for £80 a course. Well, more power to you Richard Bertinet.

Whenever you search Google for someone to help you out whether it is fixing your car of baking bread, you tend to go with the first hits. That's because, Google has declared them, through its mysterious algorithms, the 'world expert' or the 'world leader', and we take this for granted now. Neither you, nor anyone else, bothers to dig down past the 3rd or 4th pages, let alone to the $14{,}568^{th}$. Google has de-facto declared them losers. They are not the world expert; hence you have no interest in what they are offering. But you can do for yourself what Google does. Declare yourself the world leader in whatever field you have chosen as your own. And why not?

I started working for Stenbeck, building out TV networks based on this one very simple idea I had had, one reporter, one camera. Such a simple idea. Simple ideas work the best, as it turns out. It was so simple in fact, this idea of a Video Journalist or an MMJ, that you would think that everyone else would start doing it, but in fact, almost no one did. That's because most people are fearful of taking any kind of risk. A lot of people talk about what they are going to do, but very few actually do it.

If you have the courage to take the plunge into the unknown, you will find that, rather remarkably, you have very few competitors.

Now, working for Stenbeck was a good gig, and a good job, but it was still a job. As I noted before, you are not going to make your first million working for someone else, but let's call it work experience, and that is worth a lot. It is a great way to build your brand.

Let's Recap:

1. Shock Therapy
2. Hit The Road
3. Just Do Something
4. Go All In
5. Declare Yourself the World Expert

LESSON #6
YOU NEED AN ACT

Working for Stenbeck meant, among other things, living in Stockholm, which is not terrible, so long as it is summer. In the winter, it's another story.

A friend of mine, Tony Horwitz, the Pulitzer Prize winning author, sadly now deceased far too young, but then a reporter for The Wall Street Journal did a piece on businesses in Sweden. He interviewed me for the story and asked what it was like to live in Sweden.

"Open the door to your refrigerator," I said, "unscrew the lightbulb, step inside and close the door." That was Stockholm in January.

Working for a billionaire, one never knows what is coming. One day I got a call from his office. "Mister Stenbeck wants to see you tomorrow," his secretary said.

"Great, no problem," I replied. "Where and what time?"

"He's on the boat." The boat would be his yacht, Black Knight and the boat was in the Bahamas, with him.

So that meant flying from Stockholm to Miami, where I would be picked up by his private plane and then taken to Hart Island where the tender would meet me and take me to Black Knight. I was not going alone. There would be other people there from the television group.

Well, I thought, a weekend on a billionaire's yacht in the Bahamas. How bad could that be? Trust me, it is not what you are thinking. What it was, was about a dozen giant Swedes (they are all giants), drunk and singing in Swedish before they passed out. Not a great place for a 5'6" Jew.

Luckily, there was one other New York Jew on the team – Russ Kagan. Kagan was a trader in TV programs, and he was about the best in the world at it. Another 'world expert'. He discovered The Simpsons before anyone else and bought it for Stenbeck. When I got to Black Knight, Russ took me aside, seeing that I was totally out of my element.

"Welcome aboard," he told me, both to the boat and to the team.

"Thanks," I said.

Then he gave me a great piece of advice that proved seminal to everything I did after that and still do to this day, so I am passing it on to you as Lesson #5.

"They bought the act," he said, taking a pause. "And now you need an act."

It was this one piece of advice that really put me on the road to millions.

It is great if you decide you want to be a baker, and you can now spend your life creating perfect cakes, but the odds are you are not going to make a million dollars baking and selling your cakes, at least not on your own. You would have to sell a lot of cakes.

I could have had a very pleasant life traveling the world making my little films and video news reports, but the odds are I was not going to make a million dollars doing that either. If you want to take your skills set, whatever it is, to the 'next level' and make some real money out of it, then you have to, as Russ Kagan would say, get an act. People pay a lot for an act. Cooking a hamburger is lunch. Turning that into an act is McDonald's. Giving your brother-in-law advice on his career is generally a waste of time. Tony Robbins turned that into an act.

After I signed on with Stenbeck, the first place he sent me was to Bergen, Norway. He had bought a cable system in Norway (this is how it is with billionaires), and he wanted me to go and set up a local TV news channel in Bergen. Up until then, Bergen was served only by NRK, the Norwegian national television network. And, of course, as such, NRK might sent a reporter and crew to Bergen a few times a week to do a story or two. The plan was to train and field 30 video equipped reporters just in Bergen; working in this way I had invented by accident for myself.

When I got to Bergen, of course, I had absolutely no idea what I was doing. My entire experience had been working on my own, shooting my own little stories and selling them to whomever would buy them. Now, Stenbeck told me I had to have TV Bergen on the air in a month.

Now, let me tell you, this was a lot more frightening than the coal miners in Kentucky. Here, I had moved to Stockholm and done a deal with the scary billionaire, and now he was laying out a seemingly impossible challenge before me. Shades of Joseph Campbell and the hero's journey.

TV Bergen was entirely new. Stenbeck had bought the building, the gear and had hired the staff. 30 young journalists with pretty much no experience. A few had written for local newspapers, but that was about it. And now, I was supposed to get them on the air in 30 days.

In the newsroom were 30 boxes with new Hi8 video cameras, the same one I had taken to Gaza.

"Make them you," Stenbeck had told me. That was it. That was the sum total of my instructions.

Easier said than done.

I went back to my hotel to have a think. A long think.

The hotel Stenbeck's people had booked me into in Bergen carried CNN International. I turned it on. I watched it a lot. And as I had done with *A Soldier's Story*, I took copious notes. How were the news packages made? What were the shots? How much sound was used? I was up all night deconstructing them.

As it turns out, there are very few secrets in the world. Want to know how to make a great Hollywood movie? Turn on Netflix. There it all is, done by the world's best directors. Right there in front of you for free. Why go to film school when the world's greatest directors are showing you their work for free (or at least for a Netflix subscription)?

The next morning when I met with the team, I knew what to do. I would teach them to make CNN type stories, just as I had seen them on CNN. If you watch enough of the CNN, or any news story for that matter, they are all pretty much the same. The characters may change but the architecture, how the stories are made, it repetitive. The formula. The pattern. Deconstructed, every news story visually is made more or less of the same basic 5 shots, repeated over and over in different order. To that is what I did. I taught the Bergen reporters to just make those 5 shots, again and again, and a few soundbites. And it worked. In 4 weeks, we were on the air.

I had found my act.

As it turned out, it was an act I would continue to refine and perform for the next 30 years to great success. I even trademarked it. The 5-Shot Method™.

When I was a producer at WNET/13, I did a documentary on stand-up comedians. To do it, I interviewed about a dozen stand-up comics. They all told me the same thing. They all said, "you do the same 20 minutes your whole life, you just keep refining it." Every profession, every success has a repeatable pattern. Find the pattern, learn it and repeat it.

And that was what I had discovered. My own 20-minute act.

The act made my own work infinitely reproduceable. Anyone could learn it and do it, over and over. And it worked. It was like the Industrial Revolution in Victorian England. Once, stockings were made one at a time – long, tedious and laborious work. People like Richard Arkwright watched the process that an individual stocking maker would perform on her own and designed a machine to replicate each step. That was his pathway to fame and fortune. In a sense, I had done the same thing, and so can you. Make your skill, whatever it is, scalable and reproduceable.

The 30 reporters at TV Bergen went through an intensive bootcamp with me to learn how to make TV news in a very different way, on their own. I taught them the 5-shot method, and how to meld movie storytelling to TV journalism. And it worked.

Over the years, I have, like the stand-up comic, continued to refine the method and the act but it is pretty much at core the same. Since then, more than 70,000 people have attended the bootcamps, either online or in person. The bootcamps have proven incredibly effective. Most of our clients now are long established broadcasters like The BBC or CBS News. We are often working with reporters or producers or camera operators with decades of experience and often many awards.

We teach them a technique, but more importantly, we take them through a process of re-invention. They go from being a cog in a a machine to independent filmmakers. We free them and many have said, "now I feel like a journalist for the first time."

PART IV

LESSON #7 MAKE YOUR ACT REPRODUCIBLE

Howard Schultz could make a great cup of coffee. But more importantly, he distilled the process down to a few simple to repeat and reproduce steps so that anyone could do it and founded Starbucks. THAT was the secret. Making it reproduceable.

Ray Kroc was a milkshake mixer salesman who came upon the McDonald Brother's hamburger stand in 1954. He could see that they had a popular product, but they had only one location and they did it all themselves. Kroc standardized the process from beginning to end, made it infinitely reproducible and went on to build a company that today has a valuation of $154 billion. He went from milkshake mixer salesman to world leader in fast food. He re-invented himself. He had found his act.

To take whatever it is that you can do and make it simple to reproduce and then start reproducing it or teaching other people to do that. That's your act. And if you make that your act, your million is a lot closer. A lot closer. Because now you have something a lot of people are going to want to buy.

Know how to bake great cookies? You are only going to be able to make so many cookies in a day or a week or a month or a year. But distill the process so that it is reproducible and teach other people to make the same cookies that you can make, and now you're Famous Amos or David's Cookies.

Get the concept?

Once you wrap your head around this idea – take a process or a product, distill it down to its simplest form so that anyone can do it and then make it infinitely repeatable, you can see that this is, in fact the basis of just about every successful company you have ever heard of.

Jean Slutsky was born on October 12, 1923 in Brooklyn, New York. Her father was a cab driver and he mother was a manicurist. When her father died in 1942, she had to leave school and go to work at the Mullin Furniture Company, earning $10 a week.

In 1947, she met and married and married Marty Nidetch, who worked at the IRS. Marty left his IRS job and got a job as a bus driver and Jean settled into the life of a suburban housewife. But Jean had always had a problem with her weight. She enrolled in a program with the New York City Department of Health, which suggested putting her on a strict diet. But she found the City program and its clinic unhelpful. All the women who worked there were thin. They did not understand the struggle she had with food.

Instead, she had her own ideas on how to lose weight and invited six overweight friends to her house to meet once a week to share her tips and ideas and see how they all were doing. Word of her group soon spread, and more and more women wanted to attend. She soon started to charge them 25 cents each to attend.

She re-invented herself as the world expert on weight loss. She had no formal training in physiology. She had no degree as a nutritionist. It didn't matter. She found her act. On her own, and with no professional training, she had become, for all practical purposes, he 'world expert' in weight loss. She had an act- weekly meetings where other overweight people would share their stories. Then, she made it reproducible. What she could do in her suburban living room other 'group leaders' could do in their homes, or community centers or churches all across the country and later around the world.

That idea became Weight Watchers, which had revenue last year of $1.2 billion.

When I was just getting started in NY, I needed money. There was a sign posted on the bulletin board at Columbia University. It read, "Teachers Wanted, $10 an Hour." So, I answered it.

I met a guy named John who was running and SAT review course out of his apartment on New York's Upper West Side. He had about 40 students and there were 3 other teachers.

Like everyone else, I had taken the SATs when I was in high school, but what John had done was to distill the test down to its bare bones – a few simple tricks that would help you gain at last 100 points on the exam.

I learned his curriculum and I began to teach the review courses in my spare time as a student. As it turned out, I liked teaching and the students seemed to respond very well. The courses lasted about 6 weeks, then a new crop of students came in.

After a few rotations, John approached me.

"You are very good at teaching," he said. "I want to offer you the northeast franchise for my company," he told me.

I could only smile.

"John," I said. "I like working with you, but you're working out of your apartment, and I was just offered me a great job at

WNET/13 as a Production Secretary paying me $300 a week." So, I turned it down.

His name was John Katzman and the little SAT review course he was running from his apartment became Princeton Review, one the biggest test prep companies in the world. Katzman wrote a book, (he has written many) called *Cracking the Code*. The title referred to cracking the code behind the SATs, but what Katzman did was crack the code for taking his act, SAT review, distilling it down to something simple and infinitely repeatable and finding the market for it. He was, without a shadow of a doubt, the World Leader in scoring on the SATs.

Jean Nidetch could have just kept having meetings in here kitchen. Katzman could have kept running his small classes in his living room. Brian Chesky who founded Airbnb could have just kept renting out his room and his inflatable mattress.

All of these people had a small business, not even a business – more like a hobby that paid. But they also had a concept that was almost endlessly repeatable.

Now for the next step: find your market.

Katzman's market was every kid going to college every year. That's a big market. Jean Nidetech's market was people who wanted to lose weight. That is a big market. Chesky's market was people who needed cheap hotel rooms.

My market was much smaller – TV news stations and networks. But it was big enough for me. No matter the market, no matter the product, the model, like Joseph Campbell's distillation of the journey of the hero – infinitely repeatable, is always the same.

Now that you have an act, what you need is an audience, a market, and for that matter, a paying audience. This can often be the hardest part, and the part where most people fall down.

Many people have great ideas. Many people can bake amazing cookies. Many people have had success with their own weight loss diets. Many people have even rented out their couch or spare room for a few dollars a night. But what makes the difference between a $100 idea and your first one million is taking that idea, like Airbnb and then finding the audience for it. The paying audience. And not just finding an audience for your extra couch, but in finding a million people who can replicate what you have learned. What Jean Nidetch was to weight loss, Brian Chesky was to couch surfing.

In all honesty, this is the hardest part.

The Internet, of course, has made it a lot easier to 'get the word out' and to search for your audience. The Internet is free, and it is accessed by an estimated 7 billion people, but what makes it so universal also makes it incredibly competitive. You, with your great idea, are now but a drop in an ocean of other people, other voices, other distractions.

Every day, I must get a dozen junk mail offerings from people who tell me that they can improve my SEO, my Search Engine Optimization. That, with just a bit of fine tuning, and for a fee of course, they can put me at the very top of the Google Search engine because they (and seemingly they alone) understand the algorithms that Google uses to decide who goes on top.

Well, there is no doubt that the Internet is a very very crowded place.

When I search for 'Weight Loss Plans', I get an astonishing 364 million options. That's a lot of burgeoning Jean Nidetch's, and the odds are that I am not going to look at more than the first three or four. No one is.

The other 363,999,995 are probably wasting their time. What the Internet giveth, the Internet taketh away.

Once again, I can only speak from my own personal experience, and based on my own experience, the Internet is fine, (and I will talk about it later on), but I have had my best success in a far older piece of tech, and it seems to work.

LESSON #8 GET YOURSELF A TYPEWRITER

Some years ago, Lisa got me a typewriter for my birthday.

It was an old Underwood, Model 5, and it was built in 1912, the same year as the Titanic. But while the Titanic is at the bottom of the Atlantic, my Underwood is still clicking along.

I like to write on a manual typewriter. There is something emotionally fulfilling about the act of physically typing, as opposed to writing on a laptop, or now, God forbid, on a phone!

The Underwood is a great, heavy, massive machine – all steel with a wooden base; a real product of Victorian technology – like the Titanic. The thing weighs a ton. But I cannot praise enough the sense of satisfaction I feel hitting the keys; the physical act of moving actual metal typeface instead of shoving around electrons; the sound of the keys clicking and the type hitting the platen; the sound of the bell ringing and of the carriage being thrown; the actual physical act of throwing the carriage.

Writing on a typewriter, for those who have never done it, is a completely different experience from writing on a computer. Aside from the feel of the thing, once you kit a key, you are committed. A steel piece of typeface goes smashing into an ink-laden ribbon and imprints a letter on a piece of paper. There is no delete button. There is no going back. As a consequence, you have to really think before you strike the keys. It forces you to focus on what you are writing and to think ahead. It forces you to think.

What does this have to do with making your first million?

Let us assume that you have your 'act', and that you have perfected it so that it is distilled down to its simplest form, easy for anyone else to replicate. This is all great, but if no one knows what you have accomplished, or what you have to offer, it is going to remain your little secret.

In the Stanley Kubrick movie *Dr. Strangelove*, the Soviet Ambassador to the United States, Alexi de Sadisky, tells the US President Merkin Muffley, that the Soviets have invented and deployed a doomsday device. That, if the Soviet Union were ever attacked, the doomsday device would go off automatically and kill all human life on the planet.

"Why would you build such a thing?" President Muffley asks the ambassador.

"We wanted to save the cost of the missile race. It was designed as a deterrent."

"But what is the point in building a doomsday device if you don't tell anyone?" President Muffley responds.

Good point.

What is the point in going to all the work you have done so far if you don't tell anyone who you are and what you have to offer?

Answer: none.

Now, how do you tell them, and more importantly, whom do you tell?

In the world of the Internet and social media, you might think that the next logical step here is to get onto Instagram or TikTok or YouTube or run some Facebook ads and let fly. This you can do, but for the most part, this is an utter waste of time. The space is so crowded, so overwhelmed with other people and a billion other voices, that it is pretty much impossible to cut through the clutter and have your voice heard.

Now, don't get me wrong. The Internet, Social Media, TikTok, Instagram, YouTube are all great vehicles for getting your idea into people's hands and hearts, but before you do that, you need to build a base, otherwise it is just too competitive.

Take a look at the 50 most followed people on social media. Most followed is Christiano Ronaldo with 517 million followers, followed by Justin Beiber with 425 million, then Selena Gomez with 420 million and so on. Lionel Messi, Shakira, Ellen De-Generes, Barack Obama (221M) and so on. You get the idea. The first pure social media play is Felix Kjellberg (Kew Die Pie) #47 at 141 million. Impressive, but in the context of social media followers, an oddity. Social Media is great as a booster for you, but you have to make your mark somewhere else first.

So, what is the alternative? What's the first step?

Your typewriter.

Yes, really.

The bank robber Willie Sutton was once asked why he robbed banks.

"Because," Sutton answered, "that's where the money is."

Same holds true for you. Pay attention to where the money is. That is your focus.

And where is the money? Most likely not in the hands of the billions of people who are populating social media. Not really. If they had any money, do you think they would be wasting their time surfing on TikTok or YouTube? Probably not. They are having enough trouble just paying the minimum on their credit cards or trying to find that emergency $400. They may reward you with Likes, but you aren't going to be able to buy that Porsche with Likes. You need money. You want to focus your efforts now.

The key word here is focus. You want to get your idea, and more importantly, yourself in front of the people who have the resources to make you the millions you want. Now, it is true that you could aggregate a million dollars by getting a million people to send you $1 each, but that would take a very long time, and probably is not going to happen. Better to find one person who can write you that check for $1million, but how?

Many years ago, I had a business partner and mentor named Carl Spielvogel. Spielvogel was a genius businessman. Starting from nothing, he built, on his own, one of the largest advertising agencies in the world, Backer Spielvogel. A great deal of *Mad Men* was based on his life. His partner, Charlie Backer did the "I'd like to teach the world to sing" Coke ad. Carl gave me priceless advice on how to build my own business. The best piece of advice he ever gave me was "only talk to the CEO. Anything else is a waste of time."

It's true. If you can convince the CEO, you are done. By the same token, if you can't convince the CEO, then you are also done. It's quick and efficient. And you don't need to convince that many CEOs about the quality of your idea or product. In fact, you need only convince one.

But how to get in front of them? That's the problem. How do you get their attention?

For the past 35 years, I have tried to write 100 letters every month. This may seem overwhelming, but in fact, it is only 3 letters a day. Not so much. I spend a great deal of time reading trade magazines or websites or newspapers and magazine articles, looking for tiny flecks of gold, catching the light and sparkling in the dirt – that is, anything that might make me think that I could do something for them. The trick is doing something *for* them, not the reverse. This is a classic mistake. What can I do for you gets a lot more attention that what can you do for me? The relationship can be completely tangential. For example, if you are getting into the cookie making business, well, cruise ships consume a lot of cookies. So do hotels. So do airlines. I fact, if they need a lot of cookies; you can help. Maybe they never even thought about offering their guests cookie. You don't know. So, you see, lots of opportunities if you think about it, in lots of places. The more you look at it, the more you see opportunities where you never thought them might at first have existed.

So, write the letter. What does it cost you? A few minutes and a stamp? Here's one of my favorite aphorisms – **if you don't ask, then you know the answer is no**. So, ask.

How do you know to whom to write?

If a newspaper, for example, has written an article about someone getting promoted to a new job, well, you know, that is someone you want to get in touch with right away. LinkedIn is a fantastic source of information for this kind of contact. People in new jobs are always looking for their own new act that they can bring into the company. Help them out!

You could, of course, just hit Message on LinkedIn, but I bet that gets ignored pretty quickly. I know I ignore all the ones I get. You could email them, but emails are easy to delete or ignore. We all do that.

That's where the typewriter comes in.

Just as a typewritten letter forces you to think in a way that the digital world does not when you are writing it, so too does the receipt of a typewritten letter command attention in focus in a way that emails just don't.

Typewritten letters with typewritten envelopes are so rare today that they are hard to ignore.

When the Internet was new, websites garnered enormous potential because they were something new and dynamic. But today, the Internet is awash with content. There are 1.13 billion websites in the world today. Any time you get an email from someone claiming to understand SEO and improve your website's visibility, you may freely ignore it, and I will bet you do because 387 billion emails are sent every day. It takes a lot to break through the clutter, and more often than not, you simply cannot break through. There is just too much stuff. It is overwhelming.

In the 16th Century, Sir Thomas Gresham espoused what has come to be known as Gresham's Law. Simply stated, bad money drives out good. That is, if you have gold coins and you circulate paper currency, people will horde the gold coins because they perceive that they are of greater value. The world today is awash in the paper currency of content on the web – cheap and easy to come by. Your typewritten letter is the gold coin of the digital era. Because it is rare (and because it is physical and tactile), people will award it a far greater value in their own mind.

Few and far between are people who today receive a typewritten letter in the post. When it comes, it is almost as if something special has arrived. It not only commands attention, it carries with it a far greater psychological valuation for the recipient.

My love affair with the typewriter began many years ago. When I was in my early 20's, as I have mentioned, I took a camera and headed overland from London to Kathmandu, Nepal. When I was in Milan, Italy, I bought a used Olivetti Letra 22 typewriter. It was then the world's smallest portable typewriter – so small that I could fit it into my large backpack, and so I carried it with me all across Central Asia.

When I finally got to Kathmandu, I booked myself a room at the Kathmandu Guesthouse on Thamel. In those days, there were not so many tourists as there are today in Kathmandu, and hardly any cars – mostly bicycles. The streets were small and filled with the smell of burning incense and orange and purple clad monks.

My room had a bed, a chair and a table. I put the typewriter on the table, bought a chunk of hashish the size of a baseball for about a dollar, a cheap bottle of wine and a candle. I was set.

I had made Kathmandu my destination because I had read *The Snow Leopard*, by Peter Matthiessen, and I was fascinated by the book and the life that Matthiessen had lived. As a result, I sat down and cranked out a 20-odd page letter to Matthiessen, explaining that it was his book that had motivated me to come all the way to Nepal, and that he had inspired me to become a writer.

I went down the Central Post Office in Kathmandu and mailed my massive letter.

Three weeks later, I got an equally large envelope from Matthiessen! An answer!

With almost a religious fervor, I carried the letter back to my room at the Guest House, poured myself a large tumbler of wine and sat down to read.

Matthiessen had sent me back my original letter, but across the top, in large red letters he had written, "if you want to write, write. But don't write to me," and signed it, Peter Matthiessen.

At that moment, of course, I was bitterly disappointed, but in retrospect, it was a great letter, one of the best responses I have ever gotten, and one of the best pieces of advice. Write! So, I did.

Of the 100 letters I post a month, I would say that I get 10 responses. Sometimes fewer, sometimes more. But that's a pretty good average over 30 years. Now, of those 10 responses, perhaps one turns into a piece of business. Again, it varies, but that's a pretty good average. So, overall, I am running a 99% failure rate, which is fine. Because I only need one deal to run my business. If I get 12 deals a year, I am doing great. Over time it is probably closer to 6 deals a year. So actually, I am running a 99.5% failure rate. Good enough for me. Good enough because my targets are focused.

It is important that each of the letters not be generic. They have to be personal and they have to be direct. They also have to be short and to the point.

Many years ago, when I was just starting out, I wrote to Ted Turner, who was then running CNN, a relatively new 24-hour cable news network.

I had never met Turner and I can be positive that he had absolutely no idea who I was. Never-the-less, I banged out a short, succinct letter to him.

"Dear Mr. Turner," I wrote. "You make television all wrong."

It is important to get to the point right away. CEOs have notoriously short attention spans and do not suffer fools gladly.

I went on to explain how I could get rid of most of the extraneous staffing that TV news until then required. It didn't take long. Maybe 3 sentences.

Then, I came to the wrap up. This is what we call the 'call to action'. Get aggressive. Telegraph the next step.

"You give me ten minutes, and I will give you the world; or whatever part of it you don't already own."

And that was that.

Sealed, stamped and sent.

Three days later, my phone rang.

It was Ted Turner.

"You want your ten minutes, you got it. Be in my office at 9AM tomorrow morning."

And with that, he hung up the phone.

As you can imagine, I was indeed at his office the next morning at 9AM.

He opened the door. No greeting, no handshake, no nothing. Instead he said,

“You want your ten minutes, you got it. Go!”

And he hit a button on his watch.

I dove in.

“You make television all wrong,” I explained. “You have far too many people involved. You don’t need all those people. All you need to do is teach your reporters to shoot and edit their own stories, on their own....”

I was into my elevator pitch.

He stared at me.

After 2 or 3 minutes he began to chime in.

“You’re right... I know. You’re right, I know... .”

About 7 minutes in he shouted...

“Stop!”

Then he turned to his assistant.

“Get me Pat Mitchell on the phone.”

Pat Mitchell was running CNN in Atlanta for him.

She came on on the speaker phone.

“Yes?”

“I got this Michael Rosenblum here in my office,” Turner bellowed. “He’s gonna come down to Atlanta.”

Then he hung up the phone.

“You get on a plane today. You got down to Atlanta and explain all this to Pat...”

“OK!”

Then his demeanor softened considerably. He moved next to me. Right next to me. He is a very big guy. I am only 5'6". He towered over me.

"You one smart Jew," he said, and smacked me so hard I almost fell over. "You're gonna save me a pile of money."

And that was that.

That is the power of a short, to the point, typewritten letter. Sent to the right person, it is all it takes.

And that is why **LESSON # 8 is GET YOURSELF A TYPEWRITER**

PART V

LESSON #9
SHOW ME THE MONEY

Jan Stenbeck may have been a billionaire, but to him I was just another employee. And, as we all know, employees don't make a million dollars, they earn a paycheck.

What I was also earning with Stenbeck was experience and a track record, and you cannot underestimate the value of those two things.

If you want to make your first million, you are going to need what VC people call 'proof of concept'. That is, you have an idea, but an idea is only an idea. You need a working model, whether it is your idea of cookies, relatively easy to make a working model, or an idea for an entirely new kind of television news – a good deal harder to make a working model, but not impossible. Nothing is.

Now, TV Bergen was great, but let's be honest, who ever heard of Bergen, Norway and more to the point, who was ever going to come and take a look. It was great experience, but my first million was still pretty far away, although I was clearly on track, but it seemed a very long track to get there. At least I had my 'act'. Now it was time to take it on the road.

This is where all the letters come into play. As the Sage Hillel reminds us, "if I am not for me, who will be?" So, you have to become your own PR agency and promote yourself all the time. Like playing roulette in Vegas, the more chips you put down, the greater the odds on getting a hit. But the problem is, you never know which number is going to come up, so you have to play as many as you can.

After two years of living in Sweden and working for Stenbeck, a number hit. In your own quest for your first million, you are also, ultimately, going to get a hit. If you write enough letters to enough people, someone is going to give you your shot. When you get it, drop everything and go. And then put all you have into it. This is your make or break moment.

In my own case, Time/Warner, the largest cable system in the US, was going to launch their first local 24-hour news channel in New York City to be called NY1. It was an entirely new and entirely experimental move for them. Unlike ABC or CBS, they had no prior experience in the local TV news business. They were a cable company. These are often your best bets – companies who are getting into a new business and don't have a house full of 'experienced experts' who already 'know what to do'.

Paul Sagan, (the nephew of Carl Sagan the famous astronomer), was heading up the project. He must have gotten my letter, because I got a call from him. Could I come to New York and meet with his team to talk about my idea.

I flew to New York and had lunch with this core team, the people who were going to make NY1 happen.

"How many MMJs (video journalists) would you have, he asked me.

"All of them."

"And how many conventional crews?"

"None.

This, of course, is going 'all in'. You have to be completely committed to the concept or the act. No half-way measures.

As Gloria Swanson once said, "if you're going to have a baby, make it a new one."

And much to Sagan's credit, that was just what we ended up doing. Ultimately, I would train, and we would field 42 video journalists or MMJs to cover all the news stories for NY1, making NY1, by leaps and bounds, the biggest local TV news channel in New York. Most other local TV news operations were lucky if they could field 8 or 9 camera crews in a day.

I put them all through the same bootcamp training I had developed in Bergen, and then put into practice in Sweden, Norway and Denmark.

Now, we come to the money.

How much would I charge Time/Warner for doing this?

This is a question you are ultimately going to be asked, no matter what concept or idea or project you have pitched someone, and this will probably be the hardest question you will ever have to answer.

And this is the critical make or break moment that is going to move you from salaried schmuck to millionaire. But it doesn't work the way you think.

When I had been a producer at CBS News, I was making $100,000 a year, which was pretty good money for 1986. And with Stenbeck, I had also been pulling in a salary of $100K, and he had provided me with an apartment in Stockholm, at no cost. To go off on my own meant giving up all that salary security, not to mention the apartment, which was on Gamla Stan, the most sought-after part of Stockholm. Like I said, the make or break moment. But if you aren't ready to jump out of the nest, you are never going to learn to fly.

When I met with Sagan, he asked me how much I charged for my services. This was a big job. This was going to be a full time, if not more, commitment. And, from my own perspective, I had to make this work. There would be no time to think about anything else, let alone do anything else. Like we said before, All In.

I thought it might take 6 months, and as I had been making $100K, I thought asking for $50K would be reasonable.

He sat back in his chair. Then, he offered me $19,000 for the 6 months.

Like I said, it's the make or break moment.

I have to admit that this came as something of a shock to me. I had heard that Time/Warner was spending a lot of money on this project, millions in fact. $19,000 was barely lunch money to these guys. This was not what I had expected. Not at all...

"I dunno...." I said. I was starting to get scared.

Sagan looked at me.

"Listen," he said, "cut me a break and I will make it up to you with something worth more than the money. If you can make this work, I will let you bring as many people through here to look at it as you want, any time you want. The place is yours to show off what you can do."

There is an old story about an investor who is failing in the London Stock Exchange in the 19th century. He goes to Baron Rothschild pleading for a loan to help bail him out. Rothschild says, "I will give you something much more valuable," and with that, Rothschild throws his arm over the shoulder of the man and they walk three circles around the perimeter of the stock market, chatting away. When Rothschild leaves, the man is surrounded by other brokers, demanding to know what

Rothschild said and what should they invest is? He more than made his money; far better than a loan.

That was what Sagan gave me. He didn't pay me in money, he paid me in credibility, and as it turned out, that was worth a whole lot more.

I killed myself to make sure the NY1 project was a success. I put in 24 hours a day, 7 days a week, it didn't matter. And when we went to air, it was a success, and remains so to this day.

It was only a few weeks later when another one of my many letters hit their mark. Roger Schawinski was a pirate. A Swiss pirate. There were no commercial radio stations in Switzerland, but Schawinski, who lived in Zurich, had wanted to start one. A pirate radio station. So, he put up a transmitter in the Italian Alps, pointed at Zurich and began to blast rock music in the very staid banking capital or the world. And it worked.

Now, what he had done with radio he wanted to do with television. Could he build a local Zurich TV station, which he was calling TeleZuri based on my ideas? They seemed to make sense.

We met. We had lunch. Then I took him over to NY1 for the tour. He spent most of the day, asking a lot of questions that Sagan was happy to answer. As I said, he was as good as his word. By the time we had finished, I had a deal with Schawinski to train all of his journalists to work as MMJs. How much would I charge him?

The experience at NY1 taught me a lot about taking journalists into this world of MMJ. I thought I could do the whole thing in 3 months, and now I had two recent graduates of the J-School at Columbia University who were going to work with me. So, I said, $60,000 for three months, plus airfare, expenses and hotel for 3 people in Zurich.

We had a deal.

OK. I was still pretty far from my first million, but trust me, even though I had gone substantially backward in my income, and was paying the rent on my credit cards, I knew I was on the right path.

TeleZuri was followed by a visit to NY1 by Sir David English. He was a Director at Associated Newspapers in London and had an idea to start a 24-hour local TV news channel in London to be called Channel One. Again, Sagan was great on the tour. When it was over, I sat with English in the Time/Warner conference room (always helps) and came to an agreement. Again, 3 months to get the station up and running. And the fees? Again, hotel and travel for the team, and this time, the fee was $360,000. We were making progress.

Zurich worked great, London worked great, and now, another of my many letters hit a target. I got a call from Kevin Klose. Kevin, later to become the President and CEO of NPR was at this time running The Voice of America, the US Government's global media and information service. VOA at this time was short wave radio, but Kevin wanted to take VOA into the world of television news.

Most Americans have never heard of VOA. That's because a piece of legislation called the Smith Act, which was designed to insulate commercial networks like CBS or NBC from taxpayer supported competition, forbade the VOA from broadcasting in the US. Too bad, because some of the best and most dedicated journalists I have ever worked with work for the VOA.

At any rate, after a visit to NY1, Kevin invited me down to Washington to tour the VOA facilities, which are right on Constitution Avenue, just up from the US Capitol. The operation was impressive, but it was also all short wave. If they wanted to reach people all over the world, they would be well advised to move to TV.

They already had had a bid from ABC News to convert them, which apparently was astronomical. I thought it could be done much more easily. Simply take all of your radio reporters, take away their tape recorders and replace them with video cameras, more or less. Kevin liked my ideas. We did a pilot test, training about 30 VOA radio journalists to work as video journalists in New York. The test went well. I did it for no fee. This is what you have to do.

Finally, they were ready to commit to a deal, to train all of the VOA short wave radio reporters to shoot, edit and produce their own TV news stories for what would become VOA-TV. I went down to Washington to meet with Ken Stern, the COO for the VOA.

I was nervous. It was now or never, I thought.

Stern sat across from me in the government office – large mahogany desk, bookcase, coffee table, couch.

“How much would you charge us for your services?” he asked me.

VOA was a big client. Everyone else up until now had been local. – Zurich, NY, London. This was worldwide. They had 165 radio reporters all over the world – from Mali to Cambodia and everywhere in between.

I took a pause, closed my eyes, and took my shot.

“$3 million,” I said.

Stern sat silently, playing with a pen.

I gulped.

I had been insane. That was far too much. I should have asked for $100,000. Maybe $150K at the most.

Stern looked at me.

“That seems like a lot,” he said.

I just spit out an answer.

“That’s for two years,” I said.

He leaned back it his chair.

"Well," he said, "that seems pretty good."

And with that, we had a deal

And also, with that, I had made my first million dollars.

Now, let's be honest here. No one was going to pay an employee of CBS News $3 million dollars. Not even an Emmy Award winning employee. And certainly no one was going to pay The Mothball $3 million. But I had left all of that behind. I had re-invented myself as someone I completely made up. But now it was real.

Years later, someone asked me where I had gotten this idea from, of travelling around the world with a camera and a typewriter. I had to think for a while, to try and remember. Then, it came to me. That moment of awakening.

I was a freshman at Williams. Still very much The Mothball. I had a friend there, a kind named Mikael Levin. There were not so many Jews at Williams so we had something in common. Levin was in fact an Israeli.

In 1973, the Yom Kippur War struck Israel, and Mikael had to return to Israel to do his army service. He had a little old car, a Simca, and he asked me if I would drive it to NY and give it to his parents to hold onto until he came back.

I said, sure.

So, I drove the car down to NY, and parked it in front of his parents' home. They lived on Central Park West, in one of those giant, rambling apartments. I had never been in one before.

The doorman took me up in the elevator and deposited me in front of their massive black door. I rang the bell and a friendly, white haired man invited me in.

His name was Meyer Levin, he was Mikael's father and a very famous author and journalist.

He took the car keys and escorted me through their apartment to his study. I had never been in an apartment like this – Persian rugs, wood floors, original art on the walls. I had also never been in a study. It was book lined – wall to wall, floor to ceiling. He had a table set in the middle of it, with a typewriter, and piles of papers. And a camera. There were photographs of him all over the room. In Sudan. In Egypt. In Israel. In Iran. In India.

We talked for about an hour, and he told me all about his life as a world-travelling journalist and author. And then I left.

That one hour had a massive impact on me. If you came to see me here in England, in my country house, I would take you into my own library. Book lined, floor to ceiling, wall to wall, with a lovely wooden desk, ca. 1805 in the center of the room. On the desk, a typewriter and piles of papers and pictures from all over the world.

Meyer Levin had been my model of who I wanted to be and how I wanted to live my life. I did not realize it until much later, but in that one hour, Meyer Levin had given me a model for the way that I might re-invent my own life. And that is exactly what I did.

Let's Recap

1. You Need an Act
2. Make the Act Reproduceable
3. Get a Typewriter
4. Show Me the Money

A BIT OF ADVICE MOVING FORWARD

Now, before you go, let's talk about money.

There is an old expression that says, 'the first million is the hardest'.

This turns out to be true in a way, but not for the reasons you might think.

The first million is not all that hard to get. The hardest part is, after that, letting go of the things that you 'believed' to be true and instead embrace a different way of thinking and working. It's the re-invention part. It is embracing and not just believing in; but becoming the persona you have created.

There is a tendency at this point to backslide, to think, 'well, OK, I made it, now back to my old self.' Like Hernando Cortez burning his ships upon his arrival in the New World, there is no going back. Ever.

What makes the succeeding millions much easier to come by, if you want them, is that after you get the first million, you now believe that you now believe that the persona that you made up one day is you. And it actually is.

It is this sense of self-confidence; this sense of what you now believe yourself to be that makes all the difference. The fact is that you were always worth a million dollars or more; it was always within you. You always had that Human Capital we talked about in the beginning of this book. You just had to learn how to get in touch with it; how to unlock it. Once you have done this, succeeding millions are much easier to come by, if you want them.

You did not manufacture a fake identity, what you actually did was to shed the false identity that was foisted upon you since you were a child. You are now free to become the person you always wanted to be and should have been. This is renaissance, rebirth, in the truest sense of the word.

The money is at the end of the day merely confirmation that you have escaped the past into which you had been born and the 'new you' is who you actually now are. It is a reflection of the true worth of you, as you are supposed to be.

After I did the deal with the Voice of America, I came home to New York and called my bank. The Chase Manhattan Bank, where I had banked for years, in those days had a number you could call that would tell you your balance. It was a very early iteration of computer-generated services, long before the Internet.

For most of my life, my bank balance had been pretty low, like most people's; a few hundred dollars and on rare occasions, breaking $1,000. But those were rare and generally wiped out by the monthly bills. One month into the VOA deal, I called the Chase number, tapped in my account number and hit the # sign. The computer-generated voice came on. "Your current balance is one hundred eighteen thousand, nine hundred forty-two dollars and eighteen cents."

I stared at the phone for a long time. Then I hung up and dialed it again. And then I did it again. Then I sat down, poured myself a drink and allowed myself to wallow, not so much in my new wealth, but rather in my new understanding of who I was and what I was worth.

The Mothball was dead.

You come to believe in yourself. You come to think of yourself as someone who is worth charging a million dollars, or in this case, a million and half dollars a year for your services. And you can get it.

What does the million dollars buy you?

I said at the beginning of this book that a million dollars is not a lot, but it will buy you freedom from anxiety for the rest of your life. It also buys you something else. It buys you freedom from the society- imposed limitations on your own ability and your own perception of yourself.

From the very first day in grade school, you were taught that your job was to follow the rules and be a good student or employee. This oppressive belief has crushed your own innate ability to succeed. The ability was always there, it always has been. This achievement of making your first million frees you from that self -imposed and society-imposed constraint. You are now free to do whatever you want, to achieve whatever you can imagine. There is no long anything or anyone (and it was mostly you), holding you back.

THE HUNT – SHOULD YOU WANT TO CONTINUE

If you choose to take a salaried job and spend the rest of your life as an employee, there is a great deal of security in that (like becoming a Navy SEAL). Once you are in, you are pretty much in (unless you do something terrible and face court martial).

My dad, as I mentioned, came from a military background. He and his brother went to The Citadel, the

'West Point of the South'. There he learned not just how to fold socks and dress, but to follow orders. So long as you keep following orders, you will be fine. As they used to say a long time ago, no one ever got fired for buying IBM. A long time ago.

But if you are out on your own, it's a very different world. You are a hunter. You are constantly on the hunt for the next meal.

This, by the way, comports nicely with your very deeply and until now largely repressed DNA. Homo Sapiens, as a species, spent most of their existence on earth as hunters. It is something that has a great deal of appeal to us as humans.

You can fulfill this need to hunt shooting small animals or you can fulfill it bagging million-dollar deals. Personally, I opt for the latter.

The project you are working on, no matter what the project, has a limited lifespan, and so, even while you strive to deliver the best product you can for your client, your real focus has to be on finding the next meal.

I would say that over the past 35 years, I have probably spent 35% of my time delivering for the current clients, but 65% of my time finding the next meal or deal.

Finding the next meal is hard work. In my own case, it takes about a year from initial contact (those type written letters) to starting work. That's a long lead time, so you cannot wait until the last minute!

That having been said, there is nothing so satisfying as the hunt, finding a target, getting first contact, making the pitch and in the end, finally closing the deal. Nothing. So, do not be afraid. Go all in. Write to anyone and everyone you can think of and find. You never know what is going to lead to what. One thing is for sure – if you don't write that letter, you can be sure that nothing is going to happen. So, go for it. All the time.

Here's an important point to make. This is a full- time job. I mean, full time. We tell the people who work for us, 'if you don't show up for work on Saturday, don't bother coming in on Sunday'. This is not for everyone. It requires a total commitment to success. If you are the kind of person who would rather quit at 5PM and play golf on Saturdays, that's fine, but this kind of life is not for you.

In the years that followed the Voice of America, I was fortunate to have had many opportunities afforded me. There is a belief that ideas chase money. In my own experience, it is money that chases ideas.

I have never had to advertise. I am not concerned with SEO or posting daily on Instagram or TikTok or YouTube. With 1.9 billion users on TikTok it is a very crowded space. My clients, those CEOs probably aren't on TikTok or Instagram anyway.

After the Voice of America, I was invited to give a speech at Newsworld, a yearly conference. It was being held in Barcelona that year, and in the audience was Greg Dyke, who was the Director General of The BBC. He heard my ideas and invited me to come to London and address his staff, which I did.

After my little talk, he asked me how we could proceed together. I told him that I wanted him to give me 25 of his news staff – anyone he liked, but I wanted them for three weeks and I wanted to be left alone. I sequestered them in a hotel in Birmingham, England and no one was allowed to leave -and no BBC management was allowed in. It was a bit like EST, the old 60's West Coast phenomenon. For three weeks, they all shot and edited stories on their own, over and over. In the evenings we would have what I called 'public praise / public humiliation' sessions. It made people work hard because it was now competitive.

What I tried to do in that training, and in every bootcamp that has succeeded it, is to do for the participants what all those good people did for me – to take them through a re-invention.

I always start the sessions by saying, "I need you to forget everything you know or you think you know (about TV news in this case). From now on, the only thing you know is what I tell you, and if I don't tell you, it does not exist."

This is the process of getting rid of a lifetime of baggage that holds you back. We have to start from scratch. And then, we take each participant through a process of re-invention. "You are no longer employees producing a 'news package', you are filmmakers, like Spielberg or Kubrick creating films about real people and real events."

When the 3 weeks were over, Dyke came to see the results. They were astonishingly good. It is amazong what people can produce once you liberate them to create. On the basis of that, he signed me to a 5-year deal with The BBC during which time I put 1400 BBC staffers through the bootcamps, and also met my wife, Lisa who was an executive there.

The success at The BBC of course opened the door to broadcasters all over the world, and I was inundated with requests and projects. Lisa became both my wife and business partner, and together we traveled the world running bootcamps and building or restructuring networks and newspapers.

At some point, I sold 51% of one of my companies to the New York Times and became both founder and first President of New York Times Television, which I built into the largest non-fiction TV production company on the East Coast in just two years, producing hundreds of hours of some of the highest rated TV series on cable, and of course, always using 'the technique.'

Some years later, we opened a video bar/café on New York's Lower East side, just across the street from CBGB, the birthplace of Punk. One day, Al Gore, who had just lost the election for the Presidency wandered in. He said he wanted to start a new TV channel that would be about history or politics.

I told him that there was a revolution going on; that people were making all their own stuff. That had been the whole idea behind the bar – a physical place where you could make videos and films. Based on that idea, and what he could see at my place, we started Current TV, the first TV channel totally devoted to User Generated material.

Seven years later, we sold it for $500m, which just goes to show you the importance of an act.

If you have created your new persona; you have found your 'act'; you have made your act reproducible then you are there. If, then, you can create a real-world and equally repeatable participatory event, in real life or online, like the Weight Watcher meetings or the Weightwatcher classes or the Bootcamps, then I think you are on your way to achieving whatever it is you want to accomplish.

In the now 35 years since I first set foot in the Jabalya Refugee Camp with my little video camera, much of the world has changed. The technology for participation, thanks to the Internet has exploded. It is now possible for you, or anyone else, to get your message into more than 4 billion homes at absolutely no cost.

The phone that you have, whether it's an Android or an iPhone, is, of course, much more than a phone. It's predominant feature now is its camera. It allows you to shoot broadcast quality video (4K), edit, add music, graphics and effects and go live from anywhere in the world at no cost. A decade or so ago, that same media firepower would have cost you $10 million.

Whatever your act is, the combination of the phone and the Internet have created an entirely new world and have opened the door to limitless opportunities. Anyone can do this. Anyone. Anyone at all.

All you have to do is believe. And then just do it.

FINAL NOTES

My grandparents were immigrants to America and the children of immigrants.

They came from Eastern Europe with nothing in their pockets, just before the turn of the 20th century. My paternal grandparents came from Russia in 1896. At the age of 17, my great grandmother left the pogroms of Russia and walked across Europe to Germany. She got a job as a maid in a hotel in Hamburg and worked there for year until she had enough money to pay for a one-way steerage ticket to New York. (The journey of the hero). My paternal grandparents grew up in New York's Lower East side. They were crowded into tenements, often a dozen to a room. They met at the Henry Street Settlement House. They were poor.

My maternal grandparents were even worse off. My grandfather came to America at the age of 3 from Hungary. His parents died soon after and he was raised in an orphanage in New York City, in the days when an orphanage meant an iron cot and little else. They threw him out at the age of 16 and he went to work.

Two generations later, I find myself, often quite to my own surprise, living in a Manor House in the rather bucolic English countryside, with another apartment on top of the Museum of Modern Art in Manhattan, for the few times a year we go back to NY. It is a rather remarkable and almost incomprehensible transition.

If I could do this, then so can you. Anyone can.

Will money buy you happiness?

That, I suppose, is up to you. But one thing I can tell you is, it certainly doesn't hurt.

Good luck.

And if you ever have any questions, don't hesitate to get I touch. I am always happy to help. It's my way of paying back to all the people who helped me along the way.

CODA

I began these lessons by talking about Admiral McRaven's 144 page guide on how to live your life, based on his experience as a Navy SEAL.

When the book came out in 2017, it was #1 on the NY Times Best Seller list, and spent 33 weeks there. The Admiral has since sold more than 1 million copies of the book. If the Admiral pocketed $5 per copy, (my guess is slightly more) than he has earned more than $5 million from just book sales – let alone speaking engagements and such.

As we said in the beginning, one does not make a lot of money in the military, but the Admiral long ago passed the $1 million mark with ease. And how did he do it? Ironically, it was not by following his own very good advice about making your bed. Rather, and perhaps without realizing it, he followed mine. He very much declared himself to be a 'world expert' on how to run your life, then made it repeatable by this book and its 10 steps.

Made in the USA
Coppell, TX
25 February 2025